AF137733

# Empowering Teachers, Improving Schools

Laura McPhee

# Empowering Teachers, Improving Schools

Belonging, psychological safety
and school improvement

**S Sage**

3rd Floor, HYLO
103–105 Bunhill Row
London, EC1Y 8LZ

2455 Teller Road
Thousand Oaks
California 91320

10th Floor, Emaar Capital Tower 2
MG Road, Sikanderpur, Sector 26
Gurugram, Haryana – 122002
India

8 Marina View Suite 43-053
Asia Square Tower 1
Singapore 018960

© Laura McPhee 2026

Apart from any fair dealing for the purposes of research, private study, or criticism or review, as permitted under the Copyright, Designs and Patents Act, 1988, this publication may not be reproduced, stored or transmitted in any form, or by any means, without the prior permission in writing of the publisher, or in the case of reprographic reproduction, in accordance with the terms of licences issued by the Copyright Licensing Agency. Enquiries concerning reproduction outside those terms should be sent to the publisher.

**Library of Congress Control Number: 2025947642**

**British Library Cataloguing in Publication data**

A catalogue record for this book is available from the British Library

Editor: Amy Thornton
Editorial assistant: Iris Kwok
Production editor: Martin Fox
Marketing manager: Dilhara Attygalle
Cover design: Sheila Tong
Typeset by: TNQ Tech Pvt. Ltd.
Printed in the UK by Bell and Bain Ltd, Glasgow
BB0363622

ISBN 978-1-03-620659-8
ISBN 978-1-03-620658-1 (pbk)

*For Mrs. Turner.*
*If everything around you seems dark, look again, you may be the light. (Rumi)*

# Contents

# About the Author

**Laura McPhee** is Director of Education for University Schools Trust. Prior to this Laura was an experienced headteacher with 8 years of headship and twenty years of experience within the sector. She has a proven track record of leading transformational change and successful school improvement journeys across London.

Laura is facilitator for the National Professional Qualification for Headship (NPQH) on behalf of the London South Teaching School Hub and part of London South Learning Partnerships Better Futures Team. She holds a number of trustee and board positions and enjoys guest lecturing. She writes for a number of national publications and is a co-author on Harris and Morley's *Tackling Poverty and Disadvantage in Schools* (2025); she is a regular podcast interviewee, a key note speaker and has a keen interest in education policy.

Laura is a passionate advocate for social justice in education.

# Acknowledgements

First, thank you to the team at Sage for the opportunity to write a book on such pertinent themes. Special mention to Amy Thornton and Ruth Lily for all their support and encouragement throughout the process.

Thank you to all the wonderful contributors; I'm grateful you entrusted your case studies to me. You've been so generous with your time and expertise, and the sector is so much richer for your leadership.

Heartfelt thanks to my professional colleagues past and present. Iron sharpens iron! I'll always be grateful for your supportive challenge. I'm indebted to those who encouraged me to be braver and take the road less travelled. You know who you are…

Special thanks to my friends and family; we run through fire for each other.

Finally, thank you to my husband, Dave. Thank you for always saying 'yes', for speaking my name in rooms I'm not in and celebrating me (and my nerdiness!). You're my biggest champion. And I'm yours.

# Introduction

I'm sat at the back of the teacher training induction session, pretending to read the welcome pack, when a large imposing figure appears at the front. He thanks us all for coming and quickly moves on to a lengthy monologue, warning us of the perils that lie ahead. He informs us in no uncertain terms, that training to be a teacher will be the most challenging thing we'll ever have to do.

'Hmmm. Doubt that. I've beaten cancer twice,' says a jolly voice next to me, beaming.

I've been hiding in the back row with the other 'mature' students. Who, as it turns out are not so mature after all. The beaming voice is Kate, who like me, has a healthy disregard for rules and we become fast friends. We slope off for coffee.

But the introductory 'talk', with hints of a dark reckoning, is still ringing in my ear. I thought this was the beginning of a new adventure, so why did it already feel like a zero-sum game?

I was yet to realise that the well-meaning individual, terrifying us all into submission that day, was in fact preparing us for the high stakes career that lay ahead.

As educators, we champion accountability, but the absence of psychological safety, can stifle innovation, limit progress and encourage poor behaviours.

I was lucky. I was a quick learner and, for the most part I was surrounded by exceptional teams and leaders who were extraordinarily generous with their expertise and professional support. But that hasn't always been the case.

The evidence base suggests I'm not alone.

I would bet my mortgage that you, or someone you know, has at one time or another been worried about expressing their opinion at work for fear of reprisal. Perhaps you've thought twice about sharing a concern or idea? Or were afraid to ask a question? Or perhaps you've had to address unfair criticism, chastisement or social exclusion. Perhaps you've had to battle systemic barriers in the workplace?

The sector at large has been impacted. In a profession that is high stakes, a lack of psychological safety has, at times, resulted in exclusionary practice. This is amplified when weak education policy creates perverse incentives.

Now, we're also clearly seeing a direct correlation between staff engagement and pupil engagement. Unsurprisingly, when staff feel trusted, purposeful and supported. So do pupils.

However, research shows, our sense of belonging isn't evenly distributed, with disadvantaged pupils and Black pupils reporting significantly lower levels of inclusivity (Jerrim, 2025). There has never been a more urgent time to consider psychological safety and belonging for both staff and pupils.

Let's be clear, this is a well-researched field, with a robust evidence base that points to the benefits of psychological safety across industries.

Research shows that organisations with the highest levels of psychological safety are more resilient and innovative. They perform better than others.

When we remember we're people first, professionals second; we can connect the dots. Higher levels of psychological safety positively impact staff retention and productivity.

Yet remarkably, there's very little information for school leaders about how to practically apply the principles of psychological safety.

Hence, this book was borne out of personal and professional frustration.

Whilst cross-referencing the evidence base, with qualitative data from schools and universities nationally that had strong cultures of psychological safety, recurring themes began to emerge. Ten pillars or key areas of school strategy that we want to ensure are underpinned by psychological safety.

- Leading with purpose
- Belonging
- Cognitive diversity
- Learning from failure
- Professional development
- Coaching and mentoring
- Distributed leadership
- Flexible working
- Innovation
- Place-based support

Each chapter explores theory and research, containing case studies from experts in primary, secondary and higher education, with questions linked to classroom practice and reflective tasks that invite readers to consider how to apply this thinking to their own setting.

Psychological safety is the bedrock of sustainable school improvement. Without it we might be able to carry out 'quick fixes' or meet certain key performance indicators, but at what cost?

If we're motivated by the need to develop pupils who are autonomous learners, critical thinkers and agents of change, then our workforce needs to be fluent in the language of psychological safety.

This book won't have all the answers. But through sharing qualitative and quantitative data, and the work of colleagues nationally, I hope it will provoke thinking around how we can intentionally build strong cultures which are rooted in psychological safety.

Creating a sense of belonging for pupils is intrinsically linked to ensuring our staff feel seen, heard and valued. Through creating connection and a sense of purpose, we're empowering teachers, improving schools.

# References

Jerrim, J. (2025) *A national study of pupil engagement in England's schools*. London: ImpactEd Group and the Research Commission on Engagement and Lead Indicators. Available at: https://cdn.prod.website-files.com/67598d731746d234ae3577da/682d84ebff9afdaadb41c88 2_ImpactEd%20May%20TEP%20Report%20FULL_Digital.pdf (Accessed 28 August 2025).

# 1
# Leading With Purpose

## Key Terms

These terms may be of use in understanding this chapter and subsequently facilitating discussions with colleagues in your school(s).

**Intrinsic rewards** are internal and come from within the person, rather than from an external source.

**Purpose gap** refers to the strategic gap that exists between a small team of executives and the rest of the organisation. The more senior you are, the greater your ability to live out your purpose.

**Espoused theory** references the idea that the set of beliefs a leader claims to have about leadership are different from the 'theory-in-use'.

**Values** are the beliefs we hold.

**Virtues** are the behaviours that exhibit our values.

## Introduction

Finding meaning in what we do might seem like a hippy ideal or non-essential perk, but research suggests there are numerous professional advantages for those who lead with purpose.

Purpose is fuel. It sustains us and gives us the energy to keep going through difficult periods. We all expect to experience tough times throughout our personal lives and careers, but it's how we choose to respond, that determines our character and defines our leadership. When we're faced with challenges, if we can connect to our purpose, we're often able to find the resilience we need to carry on.

Evidence shows that there are personal benefits too. Those who report a sense of purpose in the workplace are wealthier and healthier (Kim et al., 2013).

Purpose is universal but not uniform; therefore, it will look and feel different for everyone. Leadership teams often expect staff to rally round the organisation's 'purpose' (or school values), without first considering how to align the organisation's goals to the individuals' goals or seeking to understand what motivates colleagues.

There's a common misconception that our purpose must be some lofty ideal. This will of course feel unattainable for most. In reality, whatever propels you forward and drives a sense of satisfaction is worthy of being described as 'purpose'. It's unique to you and therefore defined by you, and you only.

In this chapter, we explore theory and research and hear from leaders in the sector to learn from their experiences of leading with purpose.

## How Can Research Inform Our Practice?

In a recent study carried out by McKinsey on individual purpose (Dhingra et al., 2021), more than 70% of employees said that their sense of purpose was largely defined by work. Whilst this was particularly true for those in leadership positions, this was also the case for two thirds of employees who didn't hold executive positions.

Interestingly, when employees were asked if they had the opportunity to live out their purpose in the workplace, a staggering 85% of senior executives felt they did, compared to only 15% of managers and front-line workers. Therefore a 'purpose gap' exists between those in leadership positions and the rest of the employees; with executives almost eight times more likely than others to say that their purpose is fulfilled by work.

## Who Needs 'Purpose'?

We all do. Respondents to the survey (Dhingra et al., 2021), who were less satisfied and less content, reported lower outcomes than employees who described themselves as living their purpose. In fact, employees living their purpose are healthier, more productive, more resilient, and more likely to stay at the organisation. Perhaps, unsurprisingly, when our purpose aligns with our values and behaviours, it results in higher levels of engagement. There is both a moral imperative, and a practical benefit to the employer. Win-win!

This all sounds appealing... but what about the practical realities of tackling enormous and unwieldly concepts such as 'purpose'? As we so often see in leadership, it's 'big ideas' like these, which are intensely personal and open to broad interpretation.

As teachers and leaders, we probably have a broad idea of what drives our sense of purpose, and what motivates others. We want to feel useful. We want to take part in work that is relevant to our goals and aspirations. We want to know that there's space and opportunity for growth and professional development. We take comfort in the idea that we're somehow contributing to a greater purpose or a cause that's bigger than us. This is often described through the impact that our school or organisation has in the wider community. Some of us find extrinsic rewards more motivating than others, for example the next promotion or pay rise, whilst others will be motivated by intrinsic rewards because the work we are asked to do taps into our inherent interests or values. Ultimately, when these factors align, our roles and responsibilities can reinforce our sense of self and contribute to our self-esteem.

So how do we cultivate a culture where purpose driven leadership takes centre stage?

## 1  Define and Communicate a Clear Vision

Consider asking the rest of the team what parts of the school ethos or mission statement resonates with them. Learning what your employees value, is incredibly important. As a leader you have the opportunity and responsibility to help team members lead fulfilling work lives. Can you carve out further opportunity for staff to contribute to the aspects of school life that they hold dear, or that chime with their personal values? This is often where we see discretionary effort.

When new employees join, consider how to engage them in conversations about the school culture and values to find alignment. Intentionally discuss and plan ways in which their work might fit into the wider school mission.

Take time to identify and articulate your personal core values. These often evolve over time. You may want to try setting aside a few minutes to jot down your values in one column and your work duties in another column. What connections do you see between them? Can you find meaning in even small or simple tasks? What might these tasks mean to others? How does finding connection change your experience of work?

## 2  Model the Desired Behaviour

We know that it's important for leaders to follow through on their word and enact their values. Or in other words to 'walk the walk' not just 'talk the talk'.

Espoused theory describes a leader's consciously held values and their assumptions about how they behave (Argyris & Schön, 1992). These are typically the same values that are articulated in our school or Trust mission statements; statements which describe the ethos and principles of the organisation.

Our theory-in-use, however, describes our lived reality. The virtues and behaviours which are enacted, the actions and decisions of individuals and their teams.

The enacted values and behaviours that are exhibited 'on the ground' are the true reflection of the school's culture. Espoused theories often differ from theories-in-use. Some leadership teams are simply not aware of their behaviours. They're quick to articulate and encourage behaviours that align with the school's values, while their own actions demonstrate something different altogether!

Naturally, this presents challenges. It's important to understand this nuanced difference to cultivate an authentic and values driven culture where employees are encouraged to live out their purpose. Aligning espoused theories with theories-in-use is key to winning the hearts, minds and trust of employees. Modelling vulnerability, inviting alternative perspectives and facilitating cognitive diversity will help to foster alignment (See Chapter 3 on Cognitive Diversity).

## 3  Cultivate Empathy and Emotional Intelligence

It's hard to overstate the importance of emotional intelligence in leadership. Leaders with high emotional intelligence are better equipped to handle the complexities of decision-making, team management, and conflict resolution. They're also more likely to inspire and motivate their teams effectively. In fact, 90% of top performers have high emotional intelligence (Bradberry, 2014).

It's widely acknowledged that there are four main components to emotional intelligence: Self-awareness (which can contribute to improved decision-making), self-regulation (for stress management), social awareness (to enhance teamwork), and relationship management (to inform conflict resolution).

Of course, if we want individuals and teams to share their thoughts, ideas and concerns, then we need to develop a culture where they feel confident that they will be heard. This is intrinsically linked to psychological safety.

4   Integrate Purpose Into Strategy

Find opportunities to align purpose through your existing school structures and systems. This might require us to be brave and even model some vulnerability. Invite senior leaders to provide examples of leading with purpose (this could be personal or related to school) and ask them to share in these staff meetings, newsletters, school improvement or strategy days. This might include governors or trustees. Facilitate conversations for employees on leading with purpose during appraisal or during 'stay' interviews. Introduce as many 'touch' points and opportunities as possible to ensure that this becomes the cultural norm and the shared vocabulary articulating your purpose underpins key strategic documentation.

## Reflect, Connect and Repeat

When teachers and leaders can reflect on their own sense of purpose and consider how it connects to the organisation's purpose, everyone benefits.

Respondents to the McKinsey survey who engaged in this task were nearly three times more likely than others to feel fulfilled at work and able to live out their purpose (Dhingra et al., 2021).

Consider carving out time at the beginning or end of projects to build in time for reflection, enabling team members to articulate how their workstream contributes to your school or Trust's mission. You may want to engage other stakeholders such as pupils, parents and trustees for coherence.

━━━━━━ **THEORY FOCUS 1.1** ━━━━━━

### The Golden Circle, Simon Sinek

Trained ethnographer and author, Simon Sinek is well known for his theory, the Golden Circle. His theory refers to the idea that the golden circle is made up of three layers:

- **What:** The outer layer which describes what it is you want to achieve.
- **How:** The second layer which describes how you are going to achieve it.
- **Why:** The inner part of the circle, which describes why you want to achieve your goal or mission.

Sinek suggests that most individuals and organisations focus on communicating what and how they want to achieve a desired outcome, without tackling why. He suggests this is problematic because if we want to influence human behaviour, people need to understand our purpose and motivation.

In his book, *Start with Why* (2009), Sinek focuses on human nature's desire to belong. He explains this desire drives us to connect with others who share the same 'why' or purpose as us and this drive is rooted in our human biology.

The part of our brain called the neocortex, responsible for rational and analytical thought, corresponds to the 'what' layer of the circle. The limbic brain, which controls emotions, motivations, and behaviour, corresponds to the 'why' layer.

Sinek suggests that this concept is entirely transferable for schools as the golden circle concept can be used to help all organisations communicate their vision and core purpose effectively to influence their intended audience.

When individuals are asked why they chose the teaching profession, it's not unusual to hear ambitious and endearing sentiments such as 'to make a difference', 'to have a positive impact' or 'to improve the life chances for young people'. Yet as a collective, schools and trusts face numerous external accountability measures and endless education reforms, this can result in leadership teams over-communicating the 'what' and 'how' of their goals. While great systems and processes are important, they shouldn't come at the expense of the motivation or morale of the workforce. Impact is also limited when our rationale is unclear. Communicating a school's 'why' with clarity can bring cohesion and re-ignite teams.

---

## ━━━━ CASE STUDY 1.1 ━━━━

### The Education Alliance Multi-Academy Trust (TEAL)

*This case study is informed by interviews with Jonny Uttley, CEO of TEAL since 2018, visiting fellow at the Centre for Young Lives, a member of the DfE Advisory Board for Yorkshire and Humber, and co-author of Putting Staff First (2020) with John Tomsett.*

TEAL is a family of 12 schools based in East Yorkshire, Hull and York serving approximately 7,000 pupils. The multi-academy trust includes a SCITT (which is responsible for training up 80 new teachers each academic year), primary, secondary, alternative provision and a free school specialising in SEMH. Under Uttley's leadership, TEAL have become synonymous with highly inclusive education of the highest standard.

Like many CEOs, Uttley found the first year challenging, the move from Executive Principal to CEO required him to redefine relationships with school leaders while adapting to leading the organisation. Within a year, however, he saw the opportunity to rethink systems that no longer served the trust, radically shifting its direction. Guided by the Demos principle *'Don't fit your purpose round your systems, fit your systems around your purpose'*, Uttley refined his vision for TEAL – a vision reinforced by Tomsett (co-author of *Putting Staff First*), who helped instil in him the enduring value of leading with purpose.

As the architect of the trusts' renewed mission, Uttley needed to lead the charge on asking some challenging questions. As schools and respective leadership teams evolved, what role did the trust have as community leaders and as system leaders? Inspired by Simon Sinek, Uttley returned to fundamentals. What mattered to the staff body and wider community? What did they stand for? What was their 'why?'

Uttley asked the wider team a simple question: Why do you get up on a cold February morning, when you feel a bit poorly and still come to work?

*(Continued)*

He was delighted to hear the range of responses we all hope to hear: 'To deliver great outcomes for our kids', 'to make a difference' and 'to improve the life chances for young people'. But it was only through deeper conversations about staff motivation that the team defined their core purpose: helping pupils achieve well at school, and experiencing those 'awe and wonder' moments, such as visiting their first castle. This became their mission: 'We're here to make great schools, happy strong communities and make people's lives better'.

For the team at TEAL, the mission has stood the test of time and remains as true as ever. Uttley explains 'As CEO you need to be an advocate for the purpose and be unapologetic about over communicating the message. At its core, the mission is to 'make people's lives better'.

Why 'people'? 'People', is inclusive of the young adults and children that TEAL serve, but importantly 'people' also refers to a range of very important stakeholders.

Uttley is dedicated to ensuring that parents and carers receive the assistance they need through place-based support, acknowledging the power of community-based partnerships in tackling systemic disadvantage (See Chapter 10 on place-based support).

He's also determined that delivering high-quality outcomes for young people shouldn't come at the expense of teacher well-being. Recognising that if we continue to ask teachers and leaders to choose between family, friends and their career, then we risk driving exceptional teachers and leaders out of the profession.

TEAL's investment in their team is evidence-informed: disadvantaged pupils benefit disproportionately from great teaching (Sutton Trust, 2021), and research shows teachers thrive in strong professional cultures (Kraft & Papay, 2014).

The most impactful aspect of schooling comes of course from the impact that staff bring. Uttley prioritises training, development, and treating staff with decency. Drawing on Daniel Coyle's *The Culture Code* (2019), the leadership team foster psychological safety, enabling staff to take risks and learn from mistakes.

Over time Uttley and his team took the time to review each system, policy and process, ensuring that each of these aspects reflected their core purpose, and in 2019 the trust's approach to ethical leadership and their workload charter were launched.

Time was spent with the leadership team in each school to determine exactly what those ethical behaviours involved, how they translated to classrooms and what this meant for the wider community. It was this considered dialogue with stakeholders that led to a shared understanding and interpretation of ethical behaviours.

Uttley worked closely with leaders at all levels during this period and gave board members a copy of Becky Allen and Sam Sims's *The Teacher Gap* (2018) as a call to action to ensure that moving forwards systems and processes remained aligned to the trust's core purpose.

Uttley's call to action reaches beyond TEAL and is extended to practitioners across the sector. The trust has embraced accountability while ensuring psychological safety empowers staff to have difficult conversations and make tough decisions. Yet, Uttley warns, the pressures of today's educational landscape and external accountability can easily distract leaders from their 'why'. He reminds us not to overlook intrinsic motivation: 'It is far more powerful to hold yourself accountable to the community you serve'.

# THEORY FOCUS 1.2

## Maslow's Principles of Self-Actualisation

American psychologist Abraham Maslow (1908–1970) created Maslow's hierarchy of needs (Maslow, 1943), a theory of psychological health based on the premise that human need can be organised into a five-tier hierarchy. As educators we might be familiar with Maslow's principles, but have we considered how this might apply to a work or school setting?

In ascending order:

**Physiological need:** refers to our biological and physiological requirements for human survival, such as food, warmth and shelter. In the modern workplace this translates as basic pay (reflective of role), and our working environment. Increasingly schools are prioritising how shared workspaces (such as staffrooms and communal workspaces) can be improved to support well-being. How do your policies and practice support the physiological needs of all staff? For example, how are menopausal women supported in the workplace?

**Safety and security:** refers to the notion that we all want to feel safe and to be able to live and work in a predictable, secure environment. Naturally, an employee, who is concerned about their safety, will have less capacity to engage with their work. In addition to meeting employee's physical needs through health and safety legislation and policies, staff members will also need to feel psychologically safe.

**Love and belonging:** Also known as social needs, this refers to the strong biological need humans have for connection. This intrinsic need to belong must be fostered in the workplace. Feeling accepted, included and valued is essential for our mental health and well-being.

**Esteem:** We benefit from having healthy self-esteem and self-respect. Therefore, we need to ensure our place of work is one that nurtures our sense of self-worth. The respect of colleagues and acknowledgement of a job well done is important to all of us. Specific praise, celebrating achievement and providing sufficient feedback can help to reduce anxiety and uncertainty for colleagues and cultivate a supportive environment.

**Self-actualisation:** refers to deeper fulfilment. This can also be described as our need for a greater purpose or meaning beyond ourselves. Some people might also recognise this as a sense of achievement and accomplishment within their work. Understanding ourselves is considered the pathway to self-actualisation. Engaging in self-reflection may support this. What is important to you? What motivates you? In the workplace supporting colleagues to feel 'self-actualised' might take the form of mentoring and coaching. Or it may simply be communicating to a colleague the value of the work they do.

Recent research also acknowledges the limitations of Maslow's hierarchy. For example, our needs are not necessarily hierarchical. Life is messier than this! Our needs are intricate and dependent on a range of factors. Maslow's theory lacks validity across different cultures as priorities and needs can vary significantly. The expectations of the hierarchy may be limited to western societies (McLeod, 2024).

Maslow himself acknowledged that the hierarchy is fluid, and individuals might move between stages.

By applying Maslow's principles to an educational context, we are able to support pupils, teachers, and leaders to recognise their needs and create a supportive environment; one that empowers the whole school community to realise their full potential.

━━━━━━━━━ **LINKS TO CLASSROOM PRACTICE 1.1** ━━━━━━━━━

- Why are Maslow's principles important in the workplace?
- How can these principles be practically applied? Try mapping strategic actions for staff and pupils against each of Maslow's identified needs (physiological needs, safety needs, social needs, esteem needs, self-actualisation needs).
- What steps could you take to accurately identify these needs in the workplace?
- How can you work with colleagues and stakeholders to understand where improvements need to be made?
- In your current role, how could you take meaningful action and implement change?

━━━━━━━━━ **CASE STUDY 1.2** ━━━━━━━━━

## Ark Schools

*This case study is informed by interviews with Gail Peyton, Regional Director, Ark Schools, leading the primaries, secondaries and all through academies in Birmingham.*

For Gail Peyton, leading with purpose is deeply connected to her own life experiences. As a child who experienced disadvantage and spent time in the care system, she could have viewed this period through a deficit lens, but over time she drew positives from it and reflected on the resilience it gave her. As an adult, she turned to Buddhism, which provided a framework she had lacked as a child and care leaver, teaching her to take full responsibility for her actions: *'Although it was very challenging to take 100% responsibility for my actions, I also found it very empowering. It enabled me to become the protagonist of my life story, rather than a bystander'.*

This perspective has shaped her leadership, guiding her belief in the inherent potential of every person whether it's pupils, parents, teachers, or leaders. She explains: *'That's how I approach leadership – it's my responsibility to unlock the untapped potential in others'.* Gail's lived experience also makes her a deeply empathetic leader, valuing the ability to connect, encourage, and facilitate change. She describes this as *'a gift we all have within us'* and recognises that leadership carries the responsibility to help others find their purpose, emphasising the importance of valuing all interactions, even the most challenging.

The good news is that schools are the optimum environment to nurture and connect with purpose. Teachers and leaders are often drawn to the profession because of a desire to 'make a difference,' making schools the ideal place to connect an individual's values, with the organisation's mission and ensure the two are aligned. This is also where we often find discretionary effort.

Gail describes with clarity, the self-reflection and growth required of leaders when they're developing others. This involves relinquishing control and empowering others to make their own decisions and walk their own path. She explains as leaders, we're there to provide counsel. Some team members will require a more directive approach, others will simply need you to 'walk alongside them' and to be there as a helpful point of reference, gently steering and guiding.

Gail is keen to emphasise that when we talk about developing leaders, we rarely consider character development or ethical leadership. It's somehow assumed teachers and leaders are already the finished article. Although there is little discussion around ethics in leadership, when things do go wrong, most HR issues that arise lead back to unwanted behaviours or a breach of professional standards. Part two of the teachers' professional standards makes vague reference to 'upholding ethical standards', without ever codifying or unpacking exactly what these behaviours look like or how they translate to a school context.

So, it seems counterproductive not to invest time into teaching leaders how to build relationships or develop accountability frameworks which include virtues. Currently, teachers and leaders are charged with shaping children's character, without having to first examine their own understanding of character and ethical leadership!

Gail observes that as a sector, we focus on attributes that enable us to hit key performance indicators and successfully adhere to accountability measures, and yet what really counts is how you behave as a human being, because not only are we tasked with preparing children for life beyond the school gates but ultimately schools are not just for children, they include a range of stakeholders who also have the right to flourish: parents, staff and trustees to name a few.

This is not to say that pupil outcomes and accountability measures are not important. She insists they are, of course, essential. However, these ideals are not mutually exclusive. In fact, it's through the development of pupil and staff character and virtues that we achieve higher levels of self-efficacy and improved relationships, directly contributing to improved outcomes.

Gail is particularly interested in the idea of a framework for teacher appraisal informed by character education, one which gives teachers the opportunity to examine their values and virtues. Having completed a masters in character education, she explored how such an appraisal system might work with leaders at Ark Tindal. The team undertook a 'values in action' (VIA) character survey which identified their top five strengths and their lesser strengths. The report enabled leaders to identify how they positively contributed to the organisation and which aspects of their character they could strengthen. When leaders identified commonalities across teams that needed to be strengthened, they were able to work strategically to develop these areas so that it didn't result in an organisational skills gap.

Gail is keen to point out, cultures are created whether we're paying attention or not, so we may as well be intentional about it! Ultimately character education is about being able to make wise decisions and becoming virtue literate. What school doesn't want that for their leaders too?

---

## ━━━━ THEORY FOCUS 1.3 ━━━━

### Viktor Frankl

Austrian psychiatrist and neurologist, Viktor Frankl is best known for his book *Man's Search for Meaning* (Frankl, 1963) which documents his struggle for survival in Auschwitz and his path to finding purpose.

Frankl's theory of purpose, also known as 'logotherapy' is based on the premise that all humans are compelled to search for meaning. Frankl suggests that finding purpose in life, even amidst

*(Continued)*

intense suffering, is essential for us to maintain good mental health and well-being. He believed that people had the ability to find meaning through their actions or relationships, even in the most challenging of circumstances. In fact, he believed that being able to find meaning, even in the face of adversity, was a fundamental human driver, as opposed to simply seeking simple pleasures or avoiding painful experiences. Ultimately, Frankl believed that humans were capable of choosing their attitude towards any given circumstance.

At the start of his career, the Nazis invaded Austria. As Frankl was Jewish, he and his family were deported from Vienna and eventually sent to concentration camps. Frankl believed that humans were able to overcome disappointment or suffering that exists in the world through finding a sense of purpose. During his time at the concentration camps, he was forced to test this thinking and pushed to his absolute limits. However, against the odds, his resolve was strengthened, and he credited his survival to the meaning he found in the love of his wife and the sense of purpose he gained from his life's work.

---

## ━━━━━━━ LINKS TO CLASSROOM PRACTICE 1.2 ━━━━━━━

Coaches use Frankl's approach as a tool for reflection when considering goals and reframing challenges as opportunities for growth. This significantly improves a team's resilience.

- How could Frankl's principles support your decision-making or inform your leadership journey?
- Do you have a particular goal in mind? What does achieving this goal mean to you?
- How does achieving this goal relate to your personal or professional life?
- Are you currently experiencing a challenge? How might this challenge move you closer to your purpose or 'why'?
- Has this challenge taught you anything about yourself?
- What kind of impact do you want to leave on your pupils? Colleagues?
- Will your current path lead you to making the difference you want to make?

---

## Summary

Writer John Coleman explains we don't find purpose; we build it (Coleman, 2017). He identifies three misconceptions: expecting an epiphany, believing in a single purpose, and assuming purpose is stable. Whilst there are individuals who do describe such an awakening, it's extremely rare. For most of us, leading with purpose will involve some level of effort and a desire to *make* our work meaningful. Likewise, few individuals will experience a 'calling', most of us prefer to enjoy multiple sources of meaning that extend beyond the professional, our families, relationships, community work, passions and other pursuits. Finally, it's vital to understand that not only can our sense of purpose come and go, but our sources of meaning will change over time. Everything has its season and our source of passion or purpose as a young adult might change dramatically as we move through adulthood.

Coleman suggests enriching our lives by seeking meaning in all we do and embracing changing passions.

Throughout this chapter, we explored theories that empower us to do that, both personally and professionally, through articulating our 'why' and seeking meaning, even in the most challenging of circumstances.

This chapter also included reflections and case studies from experts in the field renowned for leading with purpose, driven by their 'why', ethical leadership and a determination to bring out the best in their communities.

## Reflective Task

Now that you've completed Chapter 1, take a moment to reflect:

1  Which teachers and leaders left a lasting impression on you?
2  Can you reflect on why that was?
3  How has this influenced your practice as a teacher or leader?
4  Who is championing you? Who offers you supportive challenge?
5  Which relationships will help you to realise your potential and enable you to fulfil your purpose? What steps can you take to nurture those relationships?

# References

Allen, R. and Sims, S. (2018) *The teacher gap*. Abingdon, Oxon: Routledge.

Argyris, C. and Schön, D. A. (1992) *Theory in practice: Increasing professional effectiveness*. San Francisco, CA: Jossey-Bass.

Bradberry, T. (2014) *Emotional intelligence – EQ*. Forbes. Available at: https://www.forbes.com/sites/travisbradberry/2014/01/09/emotional-intelligence/ (Accessed 7 February 2025).

Coleman, J. (2017) *You don't find your purpose – You build it*. Harvard Business Review. Available at: https://hbr.org/2017/10/you-dont-find-your-purpose-you-build-it (Accessed 7 February 2025).

Coyle, D. (2019) *The culture code*. UK: Random House.

Dhingra, N., Samo, A., Schaninger, B. and Schrimper, M. (2021) *Help your employees find purpose-or watch them leave*. McKinsey & Company. Available at: https://www.mckinsey.com/capabilities/people-and-organizational-performance/our-insights/help-your-employees-find-purpose-or-watch-them-leave (Accessed 7 February 2025).

Frankl, V. E. (1963) *Man's search for meaning*. Boston: Beacon Press.

Kim, E. S, Sun, J. K., Park, N. and Peterson, C. (2013) 'Purpose in life and reduced incidence of stroke in older adults: "The health and retirement study"', *Journal of Psychosomatic Research*, 74(5), pp. 427–432. https://doi.org/10.1016/j.jpsychores.2013.01.013

Kraft, M. A. and Papay, J. P. (2014) 'Can professional environments in schools promote teacher development? Explaining heterogeneity in returns to teaching experience', *Educational Effectiveness and Policy Analysis*, 36(4), pp. 476–500.

Maslow, A. H. (1943) 'A theory of human motivation', *Psychological Review*, 50(4), pp. 370–396. https://doi.org/10.1037/h0054346

McLeod, S. (2024) *Maslow's hierarchy of needs*. Simply Psychology. Available at: https://www.simplypsychology.org/maslow.html (Accessed 7 February 2025).

Sinek, S. (2009) *Start with why: How great leaders inspire everyone to take action*. New York: Portfolio.

The Sutton Trust (2021) *Improving the impact of teachers on pupil achievement in the UK – interim findings*. Available at: https://www.suttontrust.com/our-research/improving-impact-teachers-pupil-achievement-uk-interim-findings/ (Accessed 7 February 2025).

Tomsett. J. and Uttley, J. (2020) *Putting staff first: A blueprint for revitalising our schools*. London: Hodder Education.

# Further Reading

Bushkin, H., van Niekerk, R. and Stroud, L. (2021) 'Searching for meaning in chaos: Viktor Frankl's story', *Europe's Journal of Psychology*, 17(3), pp. 233–242. https://doi.org/10.5964/ejop.5439

# 2
# Belonging

---
### Key Terms

These terms may be of use in understanding this chapter and subsequently facilitating discussions with colleagues in your school(s).

**Psychological safety** is the belief that we're safe to take interpersonal risks. We can speak up, share ideas, questions, concerns and mistakes and we won't suffer negative social or professional consequences as a result.

**Cognitive dissonance** describes the discomfort that results when we realise our thoughts or beliefs do not align with our actions.

**Intersectionality** is the interconnected nature of social categories (for example race, gender and class) and how they apply to a person/group creating overlapping and interdependent systems of discrimination or disadvantage.

**Educational equity** provides every student with the support and resources they need to reach their full potential, no matter their personal or social circumstances.

---

## Introduction

In 1993, Goodenow and Grady defined belonging as 'the extent to which students feel personally accepted, respected, included, and supported by others in the school social environment' (pp. 60–61).

Our desire to belong is deeply rooted in both a physical and emotional need (Allen et al., 2021). Research indicates that pupils who feel a sense of community and belonging are more likely to achieve well in school, enjoy good attendance, experience good mental health and enjoy positive relationships with peers and trusted adults.

As educators we often reference the importance of creating a sense of belonging for both pupils and staff; however, there's little consensus about how this should be implemented. Consequently, teachers are less certain as to how this translates into classroom practice and until recently the evidence base explaining how this can be achieved has been relatively weak.

This chapter seeks to understand why a sense of belonging is so valuable and suggests practical ways this can be created for pupils and staff. Whilst we'll explore some specific themes, it's important to note that to foster a strong culture of inclusion, all protected characteristics for both staff and pupils need to be carefully considered. This chapter includes theory, research and case studies, to support readers to make considered choices when cultivating a sense of 'belonging'.

## How Does Research Inform Our Practice?

Belonging is characterised by Timothy Clark's four stages of psychological safety (Clark, 2020):

- Stage 1: Inclusion safety. This is the foundation for any strong culture of belonging. Pupils and staff feel that they're treated fairly and their experience matters.
- Stage 2: Learner safety. Pupils and staff are able to ask questions and learn from mistakes.
- Stage 3: Contributor safety. Pupils and staff feel safe to contribute their ideas.
- Stage 4: Challenger safety. Pupils and staff feel safe to question others, challenge the status quo and provide supportive challenge.

In principle this framework is valid for all stakeholders within our school community and throughout the next few chapters we'll explore in detail how each of these stages can be enacted in school settings.

The framework is a useful starting point and helps teams to develop a shared vocabulary; however, it should be used with caution. It's easy to interpret this framework as 'steps to success' and to infer teams are able to transition seamlessly from one stage to the next; however, there's no evidence to suggest teams operate in this way. In reality people don't necessarily make linear progress; there may be a need for teams to work on two or more of these areas simultaneously and we also know that under- represented groups may be subject to systemic barriers in the workplace that are reflective of wider society. These employees may feel unsafe, but are still required to challenge the status quo.

For this reason, organisations may choose to refer to the 'four domains' derived from Edmonson's research (Edmonson, 2018). This model encourages us to consider our attitude to risk and failure, inclusion and diversity, open conversation and our willingness to help to foster psychological safety; Edmonson encourages leaders to give all four aspects equal weight and importance.

## Why 'Belonging?'

Take the time to listen carefully to young people, particularly those who are most vulnerable and they'll be quick to explain why a sense of community and belonging is so important to them.

Research by London's Violence Reduction Unit (Brown et al., 2023) explored these themes in schools. While most pupils felt a sense of belonging, over a third of secondary and nearly a quarter of primary students gave less certain responses on belonging at school (answering 'yes, a bit' or 'I don't know'.)

Primary pupils valued respectful teachers and anti-bullying measures, while secondary pupils stressed the need to eliminate school violence. Both groups appreciated fair rules and felt that pressure, bullying and lack of understanding from teachers hindered their sense of belonging. Interestingly 59% of primary aged pupils articulated the importance of teachers 'accepting me for who I am'.

The urgency to address these issues is clear. We know schools are statistically the safest place for a child to be, yet suspension and absenteeism rates are rising. Last year, the overall absence rate in England's secondary schools was 7.2%, rising to 11.1% for Pupil Premium pupils and 20.7% of pupils were classified as persistently absent (DfE, 2025a). While rates of absence are lower in primary schools (5.5% absence and 15.2% persistent absence), this is still notably above pre-pandemic levels.

Suspensions are also at record levels, with 786,961 last academic year, up from 578,280 in 2021/2022. The bulk of these are at secondary level, however compared to 2021/2022, suspensions also increased for primary pupils by 27%, from 66,200 to 84,300 (DfE, 2025b).

The correlation between children with a history of suspension or exclusion from school and violence is well documented. Ofsted's report (2019) based on visits to 29 schools and PRUs in London confirms that excluded children self-report higher instances of knife-carrying.

Creating a sense of safety and belonging is crucial for successful attendance. Suspension and exclusion figures highlight at-risk pupils, with boys, those eligible for free school meals, Gypsy, Roma, Traveller and Black and Caribbean pupils being more likely to be suspended.

The discourse on supporting vulnerable pupils and the challenges schools face, particularly regarding exclusion, is extensive. Schools reflect societal systemic barriers, prompting us to question how our practices and policies may reinforce these barriers. Are we adapting the education system to meet the needs of the child, or are we asking the child to fit into a rigid model?

How can we use our community knowledge to foster inclusive education and ensure vulnerable children are not losing out on schooling or being placed at risk?

## Cultivating a Culture of Belonging

In response to these challenges the Mayor of London's Violence Reduction Unit (VRU) launched London's Inclusion Charter in 2024. This city-wide partnership between young people, schools, parents, local authorities and education specialists is rooted in an evidence-based approach and has been influenced by the young people and communities it seeks to serve.

The Charter (informed by research commissioned by the VRU) recognises the importance of creating psychological safety for pupils. It is founded on four guiding principles.

## Embedding Equity and Diversity

This presents leaders with an opportunity to explore how their systems and policies can create the opportunity for each pupil to be successful, whilst acknowledging that processes which are not equitable will do serious harm. We're required to step out of our comfort zone to celebrate our differences, challenge stereotypes and tackle racism and discrimination.

Leaders are encouraged to consider whether approaches to behaviour systems and the curriculum are equitable in recognition that we do not all have the same starting point or 'tools' in life and take deliberate action to specifically address each of the protected characteristics; ensuring equity and diversity is evident in each of our school structures including at governance and board level. This requires us to be brave and challenge traditional power structures to facilitate lasting change.

Naturally, it's important that the school's climate reflects the schools' values. Therefore, if a school purports to be inclusive, our small everyday interactions towards each other and towards pupils should mirror this. Creating a culture of mutual accountability that promotes the vision of the school community is key.

Leaders at all levels will need to be supported by systems, policies and processes that promote this aim. External reviews by leading EDI experts can provide supportive challenge here, provided they're followed with meaningful action and outcomes are shared with key stakeholders.

## Students as Active Citizens

Establishing forums for pupils and their families to share their views is essential, followed by feedback from leaders on any subsequent action taken. Easy to describe, trickier to implement!

Consider opportunities for pupil leadership that promote models of success and provide pathways for pupils to engage in meaningful dialogue with professionals about their experiences of school life. Explore whether routes into pupil leadership are equitable. Do populist voting structures mean that the same pupils are always appointed into leadership roles? For example prefect positions? Or are the breadth and range of voices from the pupil population heard? What requests do pupils and parents make that align with your school values on diversity and equity? These are the actions to prioritise.

A high premium must also be placed on co-constructing policies with the parent community and celebratory occasions such as cultural events. We all have blind spots, and our parent and pupil body are our most valuable stakeholders, providing us with the cognitive diversity needed to solve complex problems (See Chapter 3 on Cognitive Diversity).

## Being Adaptable and Reflective

School leaders are bombarded with competing priorities, as a result values related to diversity and equity are often consciously or unconsciously neglected. The evidence base highlights the importance of empowering teachers to innovate, experiment and refine their practice in response to the latest research and data, so that your curriculum sufficiently meet the needs of all your pupils. This requires us to create a culture where teachers feel safe to try new teaching approaches.

We also know that if we don't want complacency to creep in, we need to commit to regularly reviewing our practice and model being flexible in our thinking. Adaptability and refinement are key to embedding lasting change.

## Beyond Academic Achievement

As educators we also have the opportunity to direct considerable resource and energy to celebrating pupils' successes and providing enrichment activities for pupils. Creating a programme of extracurricular activities that support pupils' social, emotional and mental health, enabling them to capitalise on academic achievement. Tracking and monitoring engagement to remove barriers for pupils to access these opportunities is essential. Only then can we confidently describe an enrichment offer that caters for all groups of pupils, one that enables them to be successful in life and achieve beyond the academic.

# Rights Respecting Schools

Naturally, ambitious initiatives require investment. For this reason the Violence Reduction Unit (VRU) is investing £12m in education, working to keep children and young people in school, supporting healthy relationships and supporting speech, language and communication needs.

This includes £1.4m from the VRU to partner with UNICEF UK through its Rights Respecting Schools Award, which offers free support, training and resources to all state-funded education settings in the United Kingdom. Almost all London boroughs have signed up to the initiative to build on existing approaches to inclusion and share best practice.

The UNICEF UK Rights Respecting Schools Award supports schools to embed children's human rights in their culture and ethos. It recognises schools that place a high premium on the UN Convention on the Rights of the Child and ensures that this is central to their practice. It's based on principles of equality, dignity, respect, non-discrimination and participation. Schools taking part nationally have reported a positive impact on relationships and well-being, contributing to better learning and improved behaviour and pupil outcomes.

━━━━━━━━━ **CASE STUDY 2.1** ━━━━━━━━━

## Highlands Primary School and Uphall Primary School, Redbridge

*This case study is informed by interviews with Dr Kulvarn Atwal, Executive Headteacher at Highlands Primary School and Uphall Primary School in the London borough of Redbridge.*

Atwal described the Rights Respecting Schools Award as an integral part of the improvement journey at both schools, the 'glue that binds the community together'. He continued: 'As Principal Learning Leader, it is my responsibility to model the structures, culture and values at the school. It is pivotal that the headteacher is the lead for the Rights Respecting Schools Award and that it is well supported by the wider staff body. Ideally leaders at all levels will promote the initiative through the school's curriculum offer'.

*(Continued)*

Pupils are immersed in a strong school climate which embodies the school values. Faithful adoption of the Inclusion Charter and RRS means pupils are less likely to experience cognitive dissonance as staff 'talk the talk and walk the walk'.

Children learn to regulate their behaviours and make good choices because staff explicitly model expectations on how to manage conflict and treat each other with kindness.

Stakeholders understand that promoting pupils' social, emotional health and well-being is the gateway to accessing the curriculum and improving outcomes for all learners, in particular pupils from disadvantaged backgrounds.

Highlands has been awarded the Mayors of London's Schools for Success Award for five consecutive years. This is given each year to the top 6% of schools in London which achieve the highest pupil progress for scores for their low prior attainers.

Pupils from both settings have benefitted from the global dimension of the Rights Respecting Schools Award. The children appreciate that while they may be part of a diverse community, there is more that unites us than divides us.

The Inclusion Charter and Rights Respecting Schools have given pupils a shared language and the school community is committed to promoting the articles of the UN Convention. As a result, pupils are encouraged to become critical thinkers and play an active role in citizenship.

The school has also adopted a dialogical approach to teaching. Developed by Professor Robin ·Alexander in the early 2000s, dialogical teaching aims can improve pupil engagement and attainment through improving the quality of classroom talk and Oracy. It's widely recognised as more egalitarian than traditional approaches and pupils are encouraged to reason, discuss, argue and justify their answers to develop higher order thinking skills.

Dialogical teaching has been chosen by several local authorities as the vehicle they want to use to improve Oracy. In recognition that children with speech language and communication needs are at higher risk of poor mental health and poor outcomes later in life, the Mayor's Violence Reduction Unit launched the 'Talk Matters' programme in 2023, with a total investment of £3 million pounds over three years. 'Talk Matters' aims to identify the learning gaps for children with speech and language needs early, to ensure they get early and effective support.

A partner of the 'Talk Matters' initiative, Dr Atwal and his team host school visits dedicated to supporting school leaders launch and embed dialogical teaching and provide coaching to enable leaders to connect theory to practice.

He's keen to emphasise that schools are in danger of 'initiative overload'. For this reason, leaders will want to consider what practices have become less impactful over time and de-implement these, whilst trying to bring coherence to their teaching and learning principles. For example, there is synergy between the RRS principles which foster a sense of community and analytical thinking, and dialogical teaching which promotes agency.

The leadership team have been intentional about nurturing a sense of belonging. The RRS principles articulate pupils' rights, whilst dialogical teaching provides the vehicle for pupils to be seen and heard. When these are enacted with integrity and fidelity, we're able to centre the voice of our most prized stakeholders: the pupils.

━━━━━━━━━━ **LINKS TO CLASSROOM PRACTICE 2.1** ━━━━━━━━━━

Executive Headteacher Kulvarn Atwell describes how he has used the Inclusion Charter and Rights Respecting Schools initiative as framework for promoting diversity, equity and inclusion.

- What frameworks and systems support equity in your setting?

Kulvarn also reflects on the importance of support staff and teachers leading by example, they 'talk the talk and walk the walk' when it comes to modelling inclusive practice.

- How is a culture of inclusion modelled in your setting? How are you winning hearts and minds?

# The Struggle to Belong

When children and young people feel alienated from school the risk is that they may look for a sense of belonging elsewhere and are therefore vulnerable or at risk of exploitation. In extreme cases, this may even include radicalisation. There are many factors that can make children vulnerable to child criminal exploitation (CCE), and the greater the number of individual, family and neighbourhood vulnerabilities the child has, the greater the risk of being targeted by exploiters. There are also key moments of risk for children, such as school exclusion, running away or moving between care placements. Given that these are the very pupils that could benefit most from a strong sense of community and belonging, careful consideration should be given to their contextual safeguarding needs to ensure tailored early intervention is made available.

━━━━━━━━━━ **CASE STUDY 2.2** ━━━━━━━━━━

## Lilian Baylis Secondary School

*This case study is informed by interviews with Karen Chamberlain, Headteacher of Lilian Baylis Secondary School, leading a strategic approach to equity, belonging, and high standards for a diverse and largely underserved student community.*

Lilian Baylis Secondary school is situated in Lambeth serving a predominantly Black African and Black Caribbean student population, with a smaller population of South Asian students. The school has one of the highest deprivation indicators nationally, with nearly 60% of students eligible for free school meals. Karen Chamberlain shared her systematic approach to creating a sense of belonging for both staff and pupils, identifying five key areas school leaders and teachers can address.

### Context

Karen explains understanding the school and community context is integral. Leaders are required to ask themselves: Who do I represent? Who do I need to champion? What do I know about the community I serve? She emphasises the need to understand how your pupils are represented nationally and locally, for example Black Caribbean pupils in Lambeth are more likely to have SEN. Recognising the intersectional needs in her setting has contributed to raised standards and lasting change.

*(Continued)*

The leadership team adopted a strength based, evidence-informed approach to identify the challenges pupils faced. Schools are microcosms of society – systemic barriers to education are played out in our classrooms daily. As leaders we can better serve our communities when we seek to understand how national challenges are reflected locally and within our own settings. At Lilian Baylis this led to a deepened understanding of the barriers pupils experienced as a result of structural racism. Leaders recognised that focusing solely on exam results and teaching quality was insufficient; fostering a sense of belonging through advocates, models of success and trusted adults was essential. This contributed to pupil's own sense of self-belief, reinforcing for pupils, 'I represent success too', so that when faced with adversity pupils had the resilience and tools to persevere.

## Ethos, Values Vision

To create a sense of belonging, school leaders may want to consider whether their school values or mission statement is still representative of the needs of the community. Do they still align with your current priorities and ethos? What role did stakeholders play in determining them? At Lilian Bayliss, the school values explicitly refer to championing social justice.

Interestingly the values were co-constructed by pupils and the wider school community. School prefects led on this work and held a wide consultation across the school to ensure all voices were represented. This school year the building will be redecorated. All communal areas will clearly display the updated values which better represent the ideals that the pupils and the wider school community hold dear.

Ultimately, the school's commitment to delivering social justice and equity underpin all strategic decision-making and this is reflected in their approach to professional development and the curriculum.

## Curriculum

Lilian Baylis have spent several years ensuring that their curriculum reflects the ethnic profile of their students. Texts and library books are carefully curated to include representative authors, stories and protagonists, helping students see themselves reflected and fostering raised aspirations and enjoyment in learning. Diversity is further supported through author visits and a structured reading programme.

When it comes to assessment, the school employs a 'no grades and no targets' approach to avoid limiting the aspirations of students of Global Majority Heritage, whose Key Stage 2 results historically lagged behind their white peers. Therefore, Karen has chosen not to follow traditional target setting processes based on progress 8 projections, for fear of inadvertently capping pupils' potential. Teachers are not given prior achievement data; instead, a 'now and next' system identifies individual and cohort objectives through low-stakes progress reviews twice per half term. Lilian Baylis also bucks the trend by utilising mixed ability teaching groups in core subjects as opposed to the dominant 'ability' setting approach. Instead grouping decisions are based on the best social and learning dynamics of children. Nurture groups for five to eight children are also available where appropriate. These are taught by the most skilled teachers and a learning mentor. They're designed to be 'fluid' classes that children can transition in and out of according to need.

## Work With Community Partners

In recognition of the need to draw upon existing strong local knowledge and establish high quality partnerships, the school has taken part in a number of trailblazing projects to develop equity and deliver social justice for pupils. This is exemplified through their participation with Lambeth's SAFE taskforce (Support, Attend, Fulfil and Exceed), a programme which aims to reduce children's vulnerability to the harms of serious violence. Recently this has included fully funding the school's partnership with STEP Now, a weekly 'pop-up' barber shop experience provides mentoring, coaching and counselling for year 8 and 9 boys – a group less likely to disclose worries and at greater risk of mental health concerns. Barbers are often trusted confidants, and therefore well placed to help foster community and inclusion (Children and Young People's Mental Health Coalition, n.d.).

Lilian Bayliss have also collaborated with Flair, a technology platform focused on Equity, Diversity and Inclusion. This required the team to be willing to step out of their comfort zone and ask, 'what do I not yet know about my setting and workplace?' Surveys revealed pupils had been encountering racist 'jokes,' prompting new systems, policies and processes to address these issues and monitor closely their impact over time. The team acknowledged the key role professional development played in their journey at Lilian Baylis. Karen explains '*This meant we needed to get comfortable having uncomfortable conversations!*' High quality training remains a high priority as the leadership team continues to find innovative ways to develop the racial literacy of all staff, based on the premise that racial equality and equity must be considered a safeguarding issue.

## Pupil Leadership

Pupils have numerous platforms to have their voice heard. For example, staff regularly consult with pupils on their experience of the curriculum.

Nominated pupils attend half-termly reviews and share their perspectives with curriculum leaders. These curriculum leaders are held to account by line managers and as a result of the conferencing with pupils, there is an expectation something will change.

## Impact

There is clear communication from the leadership team that delivering social justice is everyone's responsibility. This expectation is shared right from the very beginning, during the recruitment process, so that new employees understand the social contract they're entering into.

The school's leadership team have put clear structures and processes in place to hold leaders to account. For example, as part of teacher's appraisal everyone has a target linked to tackling oppression.

The impact for pupils is clear. The work of the school community has been acknowledged by Ofsted, who graded the school outstanding in every category (2023) and recognised that leaders were relentless in the pursuit of excellence. More importantly, the school's most vulnerable pupils have the opportunity to excel. Disadvantaged pupils, Black Caribbean pupils and pupils with SEND consistently outperform their peers with positive progress 8 measures bucking local and national trends. They're leaving the setting with agency and autonomy, well prepared for life beyond the school gates.

---

## ══════ LINKS TO CLASSROOM PRACTICE 2.2 ══════

Headteacher Karen Chamberlain describes creating a culture where social justice is everyone's responsibility. Reflect on your setting.

*(Continued)*

- How are expectations around tackling inequity communicated?

The case study refers to 'removing barriers for pupils', teachers ensure pupils' learning is not capped.

- How are expectations around pupil performance communicated in your setting?
- What does this mean for your most vulnerable pupils?
- What does your evidence base tell you?

Each case study describes adaptations to school systems and the curriculum to give pupil's greater agency and to enable their collective voice to be heard.

- How is pupil voice facilitated in your setting?
- Whose voice is not being heard? What steps can be taken to include these individuals?

---

# Creating a Sense of Belonging for Staff

Naturally, we also want to create a sense of belonging for our teams. Research from Dillon and Bourke (2016) challenges our thinking by explaining that we're all able to contribute in the workplace, irrespective of our title or position at work, as we all have the capacity to exhibit six inclusive leadership traits.

## Commitment

Inclusive leaders commit to inclusive practices, they can articulate why it is important to them personally and how it aligns with their professional values. They're known for treating team members fairly and with respect. Interestingly, these leaders are also committed to the 'business case' and understand that inclusive, diverse teams that honour cognitive diversity, outperform others.

## Curiosity

Inclusive leaders are open-minded and hold their views lightly. They're curious about how others view the world and demonstrate a strong desire for continuous learning. They're adept at coping with ambiguity and in times of uncertainty, respectfully seek the views of others.

## Cultural Intelligence

Inclusive leaders demonstrate cultural intelligence and are proactive in learning about other cultures. They are equally aware about what they bring to each situation. They seek out opportunities to experience culturally diverse environments and are confident leading multi-cultural teams. Aware of the limitations of their knowledge, these professionals also ask for information on the local context, community and established ways of working. Consequently, they're adaptable and acknowledge that cultural norms may require them to adapt their behaviours.

## Collaboration

Professionals championing collaboration are highly skilled at assembling teams which are diverse in thought. These leaders recognise that it is not enough to create a diverse team and acknowledge the importance of devising structures and platforms to ensure that each voice is heard. This is set against a backdrop of strong psychological safety, so that employees feel comfortable speaking up.

## Cognisance of Bias

Inclusive leaders acknowledge that we all carry bias. As a result, they're acutely aware of their own bias. For this reason, they strictly follow processes in an attempt to self-regulate and ensure their own personal biases do not influence decisions about others. They strive for consistency and look for ways to make evidence – informed decisions to mitigate against risk. These leaders value transparency and are always on the lookout for bias (within individuals, including themselves, or across organisational structures).

## Courage

These professionals are both humble and brave. Humble because they're able to recognise their personal limitations and model asking others for support. This can feel risky in the workplace and once again, requires us to step out of our comfort zone. These leaders are also able to acknowledge when they have made a mistake. They bravely embrace diversity and inclusive practices without apology and are prepared to challenge practices which reinforce systemic barriers, holding others to account for discriminatory practice.

━━━━━━━━ **THEORY FOCUS 2.1** ━━━━━━━━

### Environment Satisfaction Theory

Urie Bronefenbrenner (1917–2005), was a Russian-born American psychologist best known for his groundbreaking work on human development in the 1970s. Bronfenbrenner believed that the process for human development was shaped by the interactions of individuals and their environment. It was this approach that led him to create his ecological systems theory. He believed that child development was made of five ecological systems and that each layer represented a different level of environmental influence on an individual's growth and behaviour. These systems are:

**Microsystem:** The immediate environment, including family, school and friends. Relationships within each system are bi-directional meaning individuals can influence and be influenced by others. For example, supportive parents who engage with learning may positively influence their child, however poor relationships with peers in school could negatively impact the child.

**Mesosystem:** The interactions between different microsystems. For example, a parent might support their child by attending weekly football matches. In this instance the interaction between the family micro system and sports micro system positively impacts the child.

*(Continued)*

**Exosystem:** External environments that indirectly affect development, like extended family and local government. Whilst a child may not have much direct contact with these individuals or social structures, they still have the power to exert influence. For example, a local councillor might lobby for better air quality and traffic calming measures near local schools.

**Macrosystem:** Broader societal influences, including economic, social and political systems, as well as cultural beliefs. For example, new technological advances or trends on social media may positively or negatively impact on children. Similarly, political decisions regarding policy and the cost of living may positively or negatively impact on children.

**Chronosystem:** Life transitions, both predictable (like starting school) and unpredictable (like trauma or loss). A child's resilience in coping with these events depends on the quality of support within their ecological system. According to theory then, excellent communication between school and parents should strengthen the development of children's ecological systems, fostering a sense of belonging. Therefore, when educators are sympathetic and take an interest in the personal challenges a family faces recognising the social or economic factors at play, this positively shape's child development. Similarly, children benefit from actively engaging in their learning, developing positive relationships with peers and trusted adults, and engaging in meaningful enrichment opportunities.

---

## ━━━ LINKS TO CLASSROOM PRACTICE 2.3 ━━━

- How might the environment satisfaction theory and Bronefenbrenner's systems inform how we engage with the school community?
- What are the implications for parental engagement? Contextual safeguarding?
- How can Bronefenbrenner's work on Chronosystem's inform our thinking around transitions in a child's life?
- What does this mean for our most vulnerable pupils? How can we offer support at school level?

---

## Summary

Educators are accustomed to operating in a culture of high accountability and high stakes. It's little wonder then, that professionals often feel compelled to choose between meeting the needs of their community and striving for academic rigour or success. However, these aren't mutually exclusive. In fact, it's through meeting the needs of the community (in particular, our most vulnerable pupils) that we're able to deliver excellence and ensure our pupils reach their full potential.

Investing in strategies that foster a sense of belonging may seem like an obvious priority, but in reality, it can be challenging for leaders to commit to this in the face of external pressures, competing priorities and shrinking budgets.

This chapter described the way in which child development is influenced by environmental factors and the role teachers can play in creating a sense of belonging for pupils.

More recent thinking and research refers to the idea that belonging is a right (Kuttner, 2023) and should not be considered a privilege afforded to a few. This is exemplified by the work of Rights Respecting Schools and London's Violence Reduction Unit.

The changes we make to practice at school level doesn't negate the need for systemic barriers to be addressed. This requires us to ask difficult questions of ourselves and at times, each other!

Fortunately, all of us have the capacity to affect meaningful change within our school setting through exhibiting traits of inclusive leadership. That may be through our work as leaders, as part of our daily interactions with one another and of course through contact with our most valued stakeholders. . .our pupils.

### Reflective Task

Now that you've completed Chapter 2, take a moment to reflect.

Research shows there is a direct correlation between staff engagement and pupil engagement (Jerrim, 2025).

1 Consider how your setting fosters inclusion safety for support staff and teachers. Do they:

  i   Feel that they're treated fairly?
  ii  Feel that their experience matters?
  iii Feel included?
  iv  Feel valued?
  v   Feel appreciated?

2 Consider how you celebrate wins, create space for new ideas and under-represented voices. How does this translate into action? How can you ensure policies and processes promote equitable practice?

# References

Allen, K.-A, Kern, M. L., Rozek, C. S., McInerney, D. M. and Slavich, G. M. (2021) 'Belonging: A review of conceptual issues, an integrative framework, and directions for future research', *Australian Journal of Psychology*, *73*(1), pp. 87–102. https://doi.org/10.1080/00049530.2021.1883409

Brown, C., Douthwaite, A., Donnelly, M. and Olaniyan, Y. (2023) *Belonging, identity and safety in London schools: Research and policy briefing on behalf of London's violence reduction unit.* London: London's Violence Reduction Unit.

Children and Young People's Mental Health Coalition (n. d.) *Mental health of men and boys' inquiry Women and Equalities Committee Written evidence.* Available at: https://committees.parliament.uk/writtenevidence/103649/html (Accessed 9 November 2024).

Clark, T. R. (2020) *The 4 stages of psychological safety: Defining the path to inclusion and innovation*. Oakland, CA: Berrett-Koehler Publishers.

Department for Education (2025a) *Pupil absence in schools in England, Autumn term 2024/25*. Available at: https://explore-education-statistics.service.gov.uk/find-statistics/pupil-absence-in-schools-in-england/2024-25-autumn-term (Accessed 18 August 2025).

Department for Education (2025b) *Suspensions and permanent exclusions in England, academic year 2023/24*. Available at: https://explore-education-statistics.service.gov.uk/find-statistics/suspensions-and-permanent-exclusions-in-england/2023-24 (Accessed 18 August 2025).

Dillon, B. and Bourke, J. (2016) *The six signature traits of inclusive leadership*. Deloitte. Available at: https://www.deloitte.com/content/dam/assets-zone1/au/en/docs/services/consulting/2023/deloitte-au-hc-six-signature-traits-inclusive-leadership-020516.pdf (Accessed 9 November 2024).

Edmondson, A. C. (2018) *The fearless organization: Creating psychological safety in the workplace for learning, innovation, and growth*. New Jersey: John Wiley & Sons.

Goodenow, C. and Grady, K. E. (1993) 'The relationship of school belonging and friends' values to academic motivation among urban adolescent students', *The Journal of Experimental Education, 62*(1), pp. 60–71. https://doi.org/10.1080/00220973.1993.9943831.

Jerrim, J. (2025) *A national study of pupil engagement in England's schools publication*. London: ImpactEd Group and the Research Commission on Engagement and Lead Indicators.

Kuttner, P. J. (2023) 'The right to belong in school: A critical, transdisciplinary conceptualization of school belonging', *AERA Open, 9*. https://doi.org/10.1177/23328584231183407

Ofsted (2019) *Safeguarding children and young people in education from knife crime lessons from London*. Available at: https://assets.publishing.service.gov.uk/media/5f5a269fe90e07207ac98082/Knife_crime_safeguarding_children_and_young_people.pdf (Accessed 9 November 2024).

Ofsted (2023) *Lilian Baylis Technology School*. Available at: https://reports.ofsted.gov.uk/provider/23/100625 (Accessed 9 November 2024).

## Further Reading

El Zaatari, W. and Maalouf, I. (2022) 'How the Bronfenbrenner bio-ecological system theory explains the development of students' sense of belonging to school?', *Sage Open, 12*(4). https://doi.org/10.1177/21582440221134089

Harris, P. R. (1994) 'Chris Argyris, Donald A. Schon, theory in practice–increasing professional effectiveness. Jossey-Bass Inc., San Francisco, California, 1992/1974, 224 pages. ISBN-55542-446-5 (paperback)', *Behavioral Science, 39*(3), pp. 254–256. https://doi.org/10.1002/bs.3830390308

HM Inspectorate of Probation (n.d.) *Safeguarding – child criminal exploitation*. Available at: https://hmiprobation.justiceinspectorates.gov.uk/our-research/evidence-base-youth-justice/specific-types-of-delivery/safeguarding-child-criminal-exploitation/ (Accessed 15 August 2025).

# 3
# Cognitive Diversity

─── Key Terms ───

These terms may be of use in understanding this chapter and subsequently facilitating discussions with colleagues in your school(s).

**Global Majority Heritage** refers to all ethnic groups except white British and other white groups, including white minorities. This includes people from Black, Asian, mixed and other ethnic groups who are often racialised as 'ethnic minorities'.

**Cognitive diversity** is the inclusion of people who have different styles of problem-solving and can offer unique perspectives because they think differently, have divergent perspectives and come from varied backgrounds.

**Bias** is an inclination, prejudice, preference, or tendency towards or against a person, group, thing, idea, or belief. Biases are usually unfair or prejudicial and are often based on stereotypes, rather than knowledge or experience. Bias is usually learnt, although some biases may be innate. Bias can develop at any time in an individual's life.

**In-group bias** is our tendency to give people preferential treatment when we identify as belonging to the same group as them.

**Ethnocentrism** is the extent to which we view the world through our own lens and perceive our own culture as superior to others.

**Egocentric bias** is our inability to appreciate another person's viewpoint which can blind us from understanding other perspectives.

**Stereotypes** are assumptions we make about others. These are often oversimplified or exaggerated ideas about a person or thing.

**Heuristics** are mental shortcuts we make based on probabilities.

*Note from the author:* The UK government, including the Department for Education (DfE), generally employs the term 'ethnic minorities' to refer to all ethnic groups except the White British group. This includes White minorities such as Gypsy, Roma and Irish Traveller groups. For accuracy when referring to DfE reports this terminology has been used. In all other instances the author has chosen to use the term 'Global Majority Heritage'.

## Introduction

How we build our teams matters. Differing views and experiences lead to better understanding and decision-making. Whilst we have made progress, when it comes to reinforcing power structures, schools are notoriously monocultural in their composition at leadership and board level. To avoid the perils of 'group think' we need to embrace cognitive diversity and develop our ability to see the world differently. Teams that are homogenous in practice run the risk of becoming insular and creating echo chambers that filter out alternate views and undermine the group's trust in those with different perspectives. This can ultimately lead to 'blind spots' or avoidable errors.

The highest performing teams embrace supportive challenge and recognise value in the ability to think critically, question and engage in honest, open discussion. Research shows that this requires diversity of thought (Edmonson, 1999). This chapter explores how we can achieve this within our own teams and foster a sense of belonging.

Whilst this chapter places emphasis on developing racial equity as a vehicle for diversity of thought, gender diversity, neurodiversity and inclusive practices in the broadest sense are also central to this conversation. This chapter will explore the science of cognitive diversity and offer practical tips on how to champion the voices of those who are typically under-represented.

## How Can Research Inform Our Practice?

The benefits of diversity of thought are more apparent at leadership level. For example, analysis by Mckinsey in 2019 found that organisations in the top quartile for gender diversity on executive teams were 25% more likely to achieve above-average profitability than companies in the fourth quartile (Dixon-Fyle et al., 2020).

Similarly, companies in the top quartile for ethnic diversity outperform those in the bottom quartile by a staggering 35%. The evidence base indicates that excessive homogeneity can result in less rigorous ideation and troubleshooting, stifling innovation and leaving critical blind spots.

Cognitive diversity in the workplace refers to the different ways in which people think. Not to be confused with the term 'diversity', a cognitively diverse workforce brings together distinct and differing viewpoints. Naturally, a person's gender, race, neurodivergence or any other characteristic can't be used to predict their preference or ability for processing and sharing information. So, it would be inaccurate to suggest that simply being a 'diverse' group is enough to perform at a high level.

However divergent perspectives can collectively process information in a way that adds value and improves performance. Hence these agendas are intrinsically linked. When we surround ourselves with individuals who are similar to us, think like us and behave like us, we are of course, less likely to experience cognitive diversity. To overcome this, we need to actively seek out opportunities to connect with practitioners from diverse backgrounds who offer an alternative perspective. American sociologists and mathematicians Hong and Page (2004) confirm that when solving complex problems, we should prioritise cognitive diversity over ability and that when making a prediction diversity is as important as ability.

# The Benefits. . . .and the Barriers!

Cognitive diversity can encourage open mindedness, improve cultural awareness, create a more inclusive environment and improve problem solving. So, what are the potential barriers that may make fostering cognitive diversity in the workplace more challenging? Simply put, our bias.

Over time psychologists have identified close to two hundred types of bias that cloud our thinking and impair our decision-making. Here we examine four that are commonly found and explore what this might mean for us as educators.

## Bandwagon Effect

Also known as herd mentality, the bandwagon effect describes our preference for accepting the thoughts and opinions of the majority of the group and our unwillingness to raise our head above the parapet when we have an alternate view or opinion.

It's useful for teachers and leaders to understand this and consider the implications when implementing change and introducing new initiatives. How could this be used to your advantage? Could this inform your ability to identify early adopters and allies who champion change?

We also want to make space and time for a broad range of opinions to be heard, including disgruntled employees, constructive dissenters and any under-represented groups. Consider what platforms and channels exist in school and how the structure of meetings can facilitate this.

## Confirmation Bias

We're inclined to pay more attention to data that confirms what we already believe to be true. Confirmation bias acknowledges our tendency to be too hasty to dismiss critical information in favour of our existing point of view.

Settings with exceptional practice encourage triangulation using multiple sources of data. This information is used to quality assure evaluations about the provision. In these settings, leaders actively seek out alternate perspectives. They sense check the data and ask themselves, 'Am I accurately reporting what I see?' and 'Are others accurately reporting what they have seen?' Robust discussions involving high levels of cognitive diversity ensue and leaders are encouraged to test their thinking to accurately diagnose the issue and devise an appropriate plan of action. Jeong and Brower (2008) describe this process of slowing down our thinking and quality assuring our 'sense-making' as a three-step process of noticing, interpreting and acting, enhanced through cognitive diversity.

## Mere-Exposure Effect

Mere-exposure effect refers to the concept that people may express preference for ideas or ways of working, simply because it is familiar to them.

This can present both opportunities and barriers for schools. For example, when implementing new ideas or initiatives, leaders and teachers can experience resistance from team members who have become accustomed to a particular way of working. Understandably given the competing priorities that exist within the school day and across the sector at large, we have tendency to lean into what we know rather than step out of our comfort zone. However, this can inevitably present a challenge for teachers and leaders implementing change.

The evidence suggests that repeated and regular exposure to the new strategy you are introducing will help to counteract any hesitation from the team or reluctance to follow the new initiative. The introduction of evidence-informed practice and research (underpinned by cognitive diversity) will also motivate colleagues to seek out examples of 'what works' rather then rely on impassioned retorts.

## Negativity Bias

Negativity bias describes our propensity to pay more attention to negative thoughts or comments and to give them more weight (Vaish et al., 2008). It's now widely accepted that this likely evolved as a survival mechanism for early humans who needed to be alert to dangers. However, in the modern world, it is arguably less useful to lend more weight to negative thoughts or events than positive ones (Carretié et al., 2001).

It's worth teachers and leaders considering how this can impact both pupils and teachers alike. For pupils, a proportionate amount of positive feedback in the classroom can help develop resilience. Avoiding generalisations and being specific when sharing next steps and offering feedback will empower pupils and reduce feelings of learnt helplessness. Coupled with a growth mindset, pupils will begin to see mistakes as learning opportunities (Dweck et al., 2014). Regular opportunities to hear from peers and learn from others will build cognitive diversity in the classroom.

Naturally, adults are not exempt, and the ability to develop our own self-awareness and manage our own negativity bias can be transformative. This might be through informal sense-making steps (noticing and interpreting before acting). Or through developing empathy for others and participating in more formal training such as conflict resolution, all of which will strengthen our resolve and capacity to take on board another person's perspective.

### ━━━━━ LINKS TO CLASSROOM PRACTICE 3.1 ━━━━━

- What practical steps can we take to identify and counteract bias in the workplace?
- How do your systems and policies actively promote this?

## Developing the Pipeline

Diversity of thought can be achieved through lessening the impact of cognitive bias. Hence the importance of making a concerted effort to collaborate with those who think differently to us. Yet all too often our schools and colleges are homogenous and if we're not careful this can negatively impact our decision-making ability.

Racial inequality, in particular, continues to be a challenge for schools nationally. Whilst we have seen a small increase in the proportion of teaching staff of Global Majority Heritage, there is still much work to be done.

The NFER's recent report on Racial Equality (Worth et al., 2022) challenged traditional thinking on the recruitment and retention crisis and brought into sharp focus the urgent need to address racial disparity.

The report revealed that applicants of Global Majority Heritage are overrepresented when applying to postgraduate Initial Teacher Training courses, suggesting there was still high demand for places. However, these groups are significantly less likely to be accepted onto the course.

The research also revealed stark contrasts in the conversion rates from Early Career Teacher/Newly Qualified Teacher to leadership roles for teachers of Global Majority Heritage, culminating in significant under-representation at senior leadership and headship level. For example, middle leaders from Asian backgrounds are 3% less likely to be promoted to senior leadership roles than their white counterparts, and middle leaders from black backgrounds are 4% less likely.

At the same time, we are seeing increasing numbers of pupils from 'minority ethnic backgrounds' (*see the note on p. 27) access education. Indicating that many pupils will not see themselves represented in their teachers. As a result, we risk all pupils missing out on the diversity of experience and understanding that race-conscious teams have to offer (Joseph-Salisbury, 2020). Some pupils, such as those from Traveller, Gypsy and Roma backgrounds, may never be taught by a teacher from the same race as them.

Yet significant evidence has emerged from the United States which demonstrates the positive impact of same-race teachers on the educational outcomes of pupils of Global Majority Heritage, particularly for pupils from Black backgrounds (Gershenson et al., 2017).

## ━━━━━ CASE STUDY 3.1 ━━━━━

## Leaders Like Us, National Society for Education

*This case study is informed by interviews with Emily Norman, Head of Curriculum and Inclusion at the National Society for Education, Leaders Like Us programme & Utha Vallade, Associate Assistant Principal and Leaders Like Us participant*

The National Society for Education (NSE) launched their flagship leadership programme, 'Leaders Like Us' in 2023. The programme seeks to develop the pipeline of leaders from Global Majority Heritage backgrounds (NSE, 2023).

'Leaders Like Us' is a multi-faceted programme lasting 18 months. The structure of this course was based on Professor Paul Miller's influential research on tackling race inequality in schools (2020).

Participants describe the programme as 'having depth and integrity'. The education team at CEFEL attribute this to the course content being firmly rooted in teaching and work of pioneers such as educators Allana Gay and BAME Ed, who have consistently championed the voices of Global Majority leaders.

*(Continued)*

The programme aims to develop the knowledge and skills required to prepare participants for headship in the next 2–5 years. It's open to teachers in all schools across England and, you don't need to teach in a Church of England school to be eligible to apply.

The programme consists of four key components:

1  Training: NSE's Racial Justice Team is committed to supporting participants find the right professional qualification for them (NPQ, NPQSL, NPQH), in addition participants have the option to enrol with training provider Aspiring Heads. The team carefully guides and tracks participants' progress throughout their training.

2  Shadowing: Participants are offered the opportunity to shadow a headteacher and senior leaders in an alternative setting for up to a week. Over the course of five days, aspiring leaders have the opportunity to experience headship first-hand and experience tasks that require both operational and strategic thinking. Day one is spent exploring the school culture, learning about school's ethos and values and familiarising oneself with key documents systems, policies and processes (with a specific focus on EDI). Day two is dedicated to reviewing the school's self-evaluation and school development plan. Participants are encouraged to focus on one element that is of particular interest to them and meets their training need. Day three is dedicated to curriculum and professional development, participants can meet with middle leaders and subject leaders to explore the curriculum in depth with a focus on representation. The fourth day is spent reviewing the school's strategy and the provision that is in place to meet the needs of all learners including disadvantaged pupils and those with special educational needs. The last day is spent exploring the school's partnerships within the community and governance. Crucially, participants can tailor the experience according to their training needs.

3  Mentoring: Course participants are also offered a mentor. The mentor may not be of Global Majority Heritage, but they must be an ally. The NSE's inclusion team ensures that mentors receive extensive training. The mentors are experienced leaders in their own right and provide peer-support for one another throughout the programme via a series of carefully scheduled 'drop-in' sessions.

4  Networking: The NSE Curriculum and Inclusion team host several virtual and in-person events throughout the programme. This enables each cohort of participants to develop long-lasting professional relationships so that they can establish a support network that endures long after the programme has ended. Participants have the opportunity to become confidantes and advocates for one another, joining together at regional and national events to celebrate each other's successes.

Utha Vallade, Associate Assistant Principal, described the impact the LLU course has had on her:

> As an aspiring headteacher, I am immensely grateful for a programme such as Leaders Like Us (LLU), its mission to increase the representation of headteachers from Global Majority Heritage resonates deeply with me. Upon reflection, I can confidently say that this has been a transformative experience. Before joining LLU, I often felt like an outsider in the education system, grappling with the challenges of breaking through barriers that come with being ambitious for our students and being from Global Majority Heritage. However, joining the LLU programme has opened the doors to a supportive

community made of trailblazers and equally ambitious leaders who share my aspirations and understand the unique experiences and hurdles we face. This sense of belonging has been incredibly empowering, reaffirming my commitment to pursue a headship role with more confidence. The LLU programme's ambition to promote diversity in education, more specifically at headship level, is not merely a goal; it is a strategic roadmap.

The programme provides peer support and mentorship underpinned by the principles of psychological safety. This is necessary to empower; prepare and equip leaders to enact the change they want to see across the sector and provide supportive challenge.

NSE are also clear that this responsibility does not solely lie with leaders of Global Majority Heritage. We all have a responsibility to implement effective strategies for pursuing equity, diversity, inclusion and justice for children and adults. This is best articulated in *Flourishing Together* (Confederation of School Trusts, 2024), which explains:

> True flourishing will also require those with power to make way for those who do not have it yet: I cannot claim to be realising the fullness of my human dignity if doing so requires me to trample on yours. (p. 9)

---

## ━━━━━━ THEORY FOCUS 3.1 ━━━━━━

### The Justification-Suppression Model

This theory explains the conditions under which people are prepared to act on their prejudices. It's now widely accepted that we're all subject to prejudiced thoughts. These ideas begin to form in early childhood and are often reinforced through our interactions with others.

Many of us will attempt to suppress acting on or outwardly demonstrating any feelings of prejudice. Why? For a variety of reasons, in part because some of us have been socialised not to and large parts of society are less accepting of these views. In part we suppress these feelings out of empathy and because they don't align with our true values.

However, individuals will also find ways to rationalise and act on their prejudice beliefs. Research also shows that when we experience low self-esteem and feel bad about ourselves we are more likely to be bias against people who are different (Sherman, 2011).

Whilst this is an uncomfortable truth, it's what we do with these thoughts, that matters.

Dr Steve Hayes, professor of psychology at University of Nevada explains most prejudiced behaviour can be explained through 'authoritarian distancing', the belief that others who look sound, behave and think differently to me may pose a threat and therefore they need to be controlled.

His team uncovered the factors that contribute to authoritarian distancing. They included: an inability to take on board another person's point of view or demonstrate empathy and the inability to be emotionally open to the pain of others (Hayes et al., 2016).

Naturally, the most challenging forms of bias are unconscious bias and behaviours which stem from privilege. Hayes and his team identified three practical steps we can take to counteract our own prejudice:

*(Continued)*

- Whilst we are responsible for our thoughts, feelings and actions, we are also the product of our culture and environmental influences. Make a concerted effort to notice decision-making and thought processes influenced by bias. Practice compassion and empathy where possible, with the expectation that when we know better, we do better.
- Take proactive steps to engage with others who hold a different point of view, particularly those you are likely to feel judgement towards. Try to sympathise with their position and then seek to understand their experience of stigma. Research shows that contact engenders trust (Pettigrew et al., 2007).
- Take proactive steps to minimise the impact of prejudice and learn how to become an ally. This might mean developing your racial literacy, joining an advocacy group, or sitting with your discomfort and yielding your positions of power to those who are otherwise marginalised.

These steps will not resolve your feelings and experiences or the experiences of those around you. However, it's important to note, if we're not acknowledging the issue of prejudice, we're perpetuating it.

---

# ━━━━━ CASE STUDY 3.2 ━━━━━

## Exeter University

*This case study is informed by interviews with Nicola Sinclair, Head of Access, Participation and Outreach at University of Exeter*

University of Exeter's leadership team recognises that fair access to higher education is a fundamental enabler for social mobility. It improves life opportunities for individuals while also benefiting the economy and society.

The university have made sustained improvements in the diversity of their student body, and have high rates of retention, attainment and progression, but acknowledge there is more to do, particularly around access and narrowing the gaps between different student groups. Widening Participation remains a priority for the team and as a result, the university have been at the forefront of innovations now widely accepted as good practice.

Nicola Sinclair describes the important role cognitive diversity has played in improving equity and equality of opportunity:

> 'Success for All' is the trail blazing initiative at the heart of the University's Education Strategy which realises the university's ambition to build a diverse, welcoming and inclusive learning community where everyone is supported to realise their potential. The team use data and evidence informed practice to identify barriers to achievement and differences in outcomes between groups, collaborating with stakeholders to address these needs and identify solutions. The team has prioritised communication; developing platforms so that stakeholders with a range of lived experiences and viewpoints can exchange ideas.

This is exemplified in the team's governance work. The structure includes several working parties that are tasked with focusing on a range of issues for example transition and induction, under-represented students and Diversity in Post Graduate Education. These groups consist of academics, student representatives and professional staff to ensure a range of perspectives feed into this workstream, challenging the status quo of traditional power structures in academia and educational settings.

This work is disseminated widely, via internal newsletters, virtual seminar series, networks that are open for all to join and via the university's annual celebration, which includes an award ceremony. This is an opportunity to acknowledge the individuals championing this agenda. Students and staff can nominate each other. As the work has gathered momentum, the number of nominations has increased from 80 to around 200. This is also an important opportunity to gain insight from education, industry or third sector experts who are allies, for example the Black Leadership Group who have driven forward anti-racist practice in the further education sector. The conference provides students with a platform so that they can provide supportive challenge to university staff and partners. The student panel is the most popular event of the conference and it's an opportunity for students to articulate what is working well and what areas of student life would benefit from more attention. Last year the focus was on the cost of living and this year students articulated the need to create a sense of belonging. Those involved with 'Success for All' have also campaigned for specific issues such as better access for disabled students on site. Nicola is clear that these events are important vehicles that centre the student experience. Her team is laser focused on ensuring this work does not take place in silo or in a vacuum, but instead is part of the daily offer at the university. As a result, a high premium is placed on embedding inclusive policies and practice. This has been achieved through developing a culture where cognitive diversity and supportive challenge is valued and perhaps most importantly, staff and pupils alike are able to share their views because this is underpinned by a strong culture of psychological safety.

---

## ━━━━━━━ LINKS TO CLASSROOM PRACTICE 3.2 ━━━━━━━

Participants in each case study refer to the importance of 'a sense of belonging'.

- How was this achieved?

Justification theory identified in this chapter, refers to the circumstances under which we are prepared to act on our prejudices.

- How are we navigating these challenging conversations with staff? With pupils?

---

# Summary

This chapter explored the collective power of cognitive diversity, acknowledging that expertise and diversity are complementary, not interchangeable skills.

When schools face new or complex problems, as leaders we should consider increasing the diversity of the group and challenge ourselves to step out of our comfort zone. We need to be brave enough to draw upon the skills and expertise of those who hold an alternate view and offer an alternate perspective. If we continue to simply add 'competent' members to the team who hold a specific skill set, we're less likely to be successful.

To fully harness the power of cognitive diversity and create a sense of belonging we need to clearly articulate the benefits.

Help your team and co-workers to understand how diversity of thought enhances the team's performance and improves outcomes, in addition to fulfilling a wider moral purpose that aligns with your vision and ethos.

We know that the most significant ethnic disparities occur during early career stages and there are systemic issues regarding progression that have not yet been addressed. However, teachers from diverse ethnic backgrounds can promote diversity of thought and enable us to view pupil's cultural capital through a new lens. When this collective force for good is properly harnessed, we have the potential to enrich the lives of all our pupils and society as a whole (Wallace, 2017).

## Reflective Task

Now that you've finished Chapter 3, let's take a moment to reflect.

1  How does cognitive diversity bring out the best in teams?
2  What aspects of school life benefit from diversity of thought? Where could this be improved in your setting? How?
3  How can we take responsibility for managing our own bias? What structures, systems and relationships will support you to do that?
4  How can you support leaders at all levels to engage with cognitive diversity and led by example?

# References

Carretié, L., Mercado, F., Tapia, M. and Hinojosa, J. A. (2001) 'Emotion, attention, and the "negativity bias", studied through event-related potentials', *International Journal of Psychophysiology*, *41*(1), pp. 75–85. https://doi.org/10.1016/s0167-8760(00)00195-1

Confederation of School Trusts (2024) *Flourishing together: A collective vision for the education system*. Available at: https://cstuk.org.uk/system/files/paragraphs/cw_file/2025-04/Flourishing_together_2024-10-18.pdf (Accessed 29 August 2025).

Dixon-Fyle, S., Dolan, K., Hunt, V. and Prince, S. (2020) *Diversity wins: How inclusion matters*. McKinsey & Company. Available at: https://www.mckinsey.com/featured-insights/diversity-and-inclusion/diversity-wins-how-inclusion-matters (Accessed 21 October 2024).

Dweck, C. S., Walton, G. M. and Cohen, G. L. (2014) *Mindsets and skills that promote long-term learning*. Available at: https://ed.stanford.edu/sites/default/files/manual/dweck-walton-cohen-2014.pdf (Accessed 21 October 2024).

Edmondson, A. (1999) 'Psychological safety and learning behavior in work teams', *Administrative Science Quarterly*, *44*(2), pp. 350–383.

Gershenson, S., Hart, C., Lindsay, C. and Papageorge, N. (2017) *The long-run impacts of same-race teachers* (IZA Discussion Paper No. 10630). Available at: https://www.iza.org/publications/dp/10630 (Accessed 21 October 2024).

Hayes, S. C., Levin, M. E., Luoma, J. B., Vilardaga, R., Lillis, J. and Nobles, R., (2016) 'Examining the role of psychological inflexibility, perspective taking, and empathic concern in generalized prejudice', *Journal of Applied Social Psychology*, *46*(3), pp. 180–191. https://doi.org/10.1111/jasp.12355

Hong, L. and Page, S. E. (2004) 'Groups of diverse problem solvers can outperform groups of high-ability problem solvers', *Proceedings of the National Academy of Science U.S.A.*, *101*(46), pp. 16385–16389. https://doi.org/10.1073/pnas.0403723101

Jeong, H.-S. and Brower, R. S. (2008) 'Extending the present understanding of organizational sensemaking: Three stages and three contexts', *Administration & Society*, *40*(3), pp. 223–252. https://doi.org/10.1177/0095399707313446

Joseph-Salisbury, R. (2020) *Race and racism in secondary schools*. Runnymede Trust. Available at: https://www.runnymedetrust.org/publications/race-and-racism-in-secondary-schools (Accessed 21 October 2024).

Miller, P. W. (2020) '"Tackling" race inequality in school leadership: Positive actions in BAME teacher progression – evidence from three English schools', *Educational Management Administration & Leadership*, *48*(6), pp. 986–1006. https://doi.org/10.1177/1741143219873098

National Society for Education (2023) *Leaders like us*. Available at: https://www.nse.org.uk/foundation-for-educational-leadership/leaders-like-us (Accessed 20 July 2025).

Pettigrew, T. F., Christ, O., Wagner, U. and Stellmacher, J. (2007) 'Direct and indirect intergroup contact effects on prejudice: A normative interpretation', *International Journal of Intercultural Relations*, *31*(4), pp. 411–425. https://doi.org/10.1016/j.ijintrel.2006.11.003

Sherman, J. (2011) *People with low self-esteem show more signs of prejudice*. Association for Psychological Science. Available at: https://www.psychologicalscience.org/news/releases/people-with-low-self-esteem-show-more-signs-of-prejudice.html (Accessed 20 July 2025).

Vaish, A., Grossmann, T. and Woodward, A. (2008) 'Not all emotions are created equal: The negativity bias in social-emotional development', *Psychological Bulletin*, *134*(3), pp. 383–403. https://doi.org/10.1037/0033-2909.134.3.383

Wallace, D. (2017) 'Cultural capital as whiteness? Examining logics of ethno-racial representation and resistance', *British Journal of Sociology of Education*, *39*(4), pp. 466–482. https://doi.org/10.1080/01425692.2017.1355228

Worth, J., McLean, D. and Sharp, C. (2022) *Racial equality in the teacher workforce*. NFER. Available at: https://www.nfer.ac.uk/media/hxpdemc4/racial_equality_in_the_teacher_workforce_full_report.pdf (Accessed 21 October 2024).

# Further Reading

Brewer, M. B. (2010) Intergroup relations. In R. F. Baumeister and E. J. Finkel (Eds.), *Advanced social psychology: The state of the science* (pp. 535–571). Oxford: Oxford University Press.

Department for Education (2023) *School teacher workforce*. Available at: https:// www.ethnicity-facts-figures.service.gov.uk/workforce-and-business/workforce-diversity/ school-teacher-workforce/latest/ (Accessed 21 October 2024).

Department for Education (2024a) *Schools, pupils and their characteristics, academic year 2023/24*. Available at: https://explore-education-statistics.service.gov.uk/find-statistics/school-pupils-and-their-characteristics (Accessed 21 October 2024).

Department for Education (2024b) *School workforce in England, reporting year 2023*. GOV. UK. Available at: https://explore-education-statistics.service.gov.uk/find-statistics/ school-workforce-in-england (Accessed 21 October 2024).

Ellemers, N. (2024) *Social identity theory*. Encyclopaedia Britannica. Available at: https:// www.britannica.com/ topic/social-identity-theory (Accessed 21 October 2024).

Hogg, M. A. and Williams, K. D. (2000) 'From I to we: Social identity and the collective self', *Group Dynamics: Theory, Research, and Practice*, 4(1), pp. 81–97. https://doi.org/ 10.1037/1089-2699.4.1.81

McLeod, S. (2023) *Social identity theory in psychology (Tajfel & Turner, 1979)*. Simply Psychology. Available at: https://www.simplypsychology.org/social-identity-theory.html (Accessed 21 October 2024).

# 4

# Learning From Failure

---

## Key Terms

These terms may be of use in understanding this chapter and subsequently facilitating discussions with colleagues in your school(s).

**Cognitive reframing** is recognising a behaviour or situation for exactly what it is, then choosing how you will allow it to affect you.

**Psychological safety** is feeling safe to take interpersonal risks, to speak up, to provide supportive challenge and to share concerns without fear of negative repercussions.

**Growth mindset** is the belief that your intelligence and talents can be developed through effort, learning and persistence.

**Metacognition** is the ability to be aware of and understand your own thought processes. Metacognition is also known as 'thinking about thinking'. It can help pupils to take ownership of their learning, plan and evaluate their learning, understand their strengths and weaknesses and adapt their behaviour to achieve goals.

**Executive function** refers to a set of cognitive skills that are essential for success in many areas of life, including school, work and personal relationships. These are the life skills that include things like planning, organisation, time management, impulse control and working memory.

**Mental models** are a person's internal representation of how the world works, and are made up of memories, beliefs and knowledge. For example, a mental model of a car will include reference to the fact it will have wheels, an engine and a steering wheel.

---

## Introduction

For all of us, slip-ups and mistakes are everyday occurrences. An inevitable aspect of our personal and professional lives. A mistake can creep in due to oversight, assumptions, fatigue or simply because of our inherent fallibility as humans.

We've been led to believe that all mistakes are costly, contributing to a wider culture of blame not just in our workplaces, but in our homes and society at large. This common misconception can in fact lead us to repeat, rather than avoid unwanted behaviours, because individuals are reluctant to 'speak up' when they've made a mistake for fear of reprisal. This is to our great loss, because mistakes, when managed effectively and with sensitivity, present us with rich opportunities to learn and take a step closer to our goals.

This chapter explores how teachers and leaders foster psychological safety and enable pupils and colleagues to thrive. It includes case studies from experts in the field which exemplify how high levels of relational trust foster innovation and build resilience.

## How Can Research Inform Our Practice?

In her influential work *Right Kind of Wrong* (2023), Professor of leadership and management, Amy Edmonson proposes three distinct classifications for different types of failure: basic, complex and intelligent (2023).

- Basic failures can also be described as simple errors – often minor or inconvenient, such as a teacher forgetting to order lunches for a school trip. Basic errors do, however, have the potential to be catastrophic; imagine a trip that goes ahead without the correct medical information and results in a pupil falling seriously ill.
- Complex errors are multi-causal by nature and arise from multiple contributing factors that align in the wrong way. For example, a serious safeguarding incident is reported to a school. However, the school doesn't have a pro-active safeguarding culture, doesn't hold up to date safeguarding training and there is ambiguity over reporting procedures, therefore the safeguarding incident is reported but it isn't acted on. This might be a more serious example; however, we regularly experience failures of similar complexity in our daily lives.
- Intelligent failures, in contrast, describe the unavoidable consequences of venturing into uncharted territory. They're necessary and important for the growth of the individual and the organisation. For example, a middle leader may have thoroughly researched a new approach to the curriculum, studied the evidence base and considered their context.

However, upon implementation, they found the results were not quite as anticipated. If we're able to reflect on this learning, pivot and move on, it can be an invaluable lesson that helps to inform the next part of our strategy or journey. Intelligent failures are the consequence of taking calculated risks. According to Edmonson, not only are these unavoidable, they're a requirement! If we aren't experiencing intelligent failures, are we being innovative enough? (Edmonson, 2023).

## The Leadership of Psychological Safety

Edmonson advocates for a 'listening' culture made up of leadership teams that are reflective and ready to learn. We're able to accept that as human beings we're fallible, and yet organisations quickly adopt a culture of blame. She proposes that in order to approach failure constructively, it's necessary to determine the cause of the error. Her research suggests, rather than responding emotionally, leaders should investigate the cause of the error and consider where this may fall on a spectrum of accountability, errors that are blameworthy, and errors that are praiseworthy (2023). This evaluative exercise is designed to prompt growth and reflection.

This work is best suited to an environment with high levels of psychological safety. A workplace where you're able to ask for help when you're in over your head and able to admit mistakes. A workplace where you can speak up when you notice something isn't right or can be done better.

The common misconception with psychological safety is that it is somehow the 'easy' or 'comfortable' option or that psychological safety removes accountability. The reality could not be further from the truth. In organisations with true psychological safety, accountability is high because employees don't shy away from uncomfortable conversations about what went wrong and how things can be improved. Consequently, there is also a correlation between strong psychological safety and productivity (Minnick, 2023). These conversations are never easy, but where leadership teams encourage this way of working, it becomes the cultural norm.

# Cultivating a Culture of Psychological Safety

So how do we cultivate a culture where psychological safety is expected, and centred?

## Develop a Consultative Approach

Consider varying the format of your meetings to enable all voices to be heard. For example, try rotating the role of Chair. All too often this position is assumed by the most senior leader in the room. Schools are notoriously hierarchal and reverting to a traditional format for each meeting can unintentionally stifle discussion.

Alternatively, when a new initiative or strategy is shared, invite team members to briefly jot down their initial thoughts and reflections and hand these to the Chair to share. This will enable new voices to be heard, encourage fresh thinking and avoid individuals dominating.

For too long leaders and specifically headteachers have been held up as omniscient, omnipotent creatures. Of course this is nonsense! We know better and the era of the 'hero headteacher' is over.

An important part of leadership, is modelling how we deal with periods of stress and challenging circumstances. In psychologically safe environments, leaders feel comfortable sharing that they don't have all the answers and model asking for help to demonstrate professional vulnerability.

As we saw in Chapter 3, the highest performing teams thrive as a result of cognitive diversity. At each opportunity, these professionals actively seek out the perspective of others through stakeholder engagement. Next time you roll out a new strategy or set up a working party, you may want to consider asking volunteers that are representative of the wider school, so that a range of roles and responsibilities are included. As a result of this exercise, it's important that the team can see how their contributions or suggestions have resulted in action.

## Create a Supportive Environment

To create a supportive environment, leaders at all levels will need to normalise failure. Whilst we want to minimise errors, we also need to accept that they can and will happen. To establish trust, leaders are required to become comfortable admitting mistakes and model learning from them. Reframing challenges and threats as opportunities will further develop the team's growth mindset and resilience.

Leaders who value psychological safety dedicate time to improving work processes and systems. This can go a long way to reducing or even eliminating some avoidable errors. Even creating and maintaining useful checklists can significantly enhance practice, particularly when colleagues help to co-produce these systems. Leaders that establish a culture of continuous learning, enable teams to make meaningful contributions.

It's also just as valuable to create opportunities for team members to 'fail safely' at something and within agreed parameters. This provides leaders at all levels with autonomy and allows innovation to thrive.

## Encourage Supportive Challenge

If you're really committed to hearing alternative perspectives, then it's important to articulate this to your team, don't assume that this is a shared belief. Be mindful that declaring your vision won't be enough to change the culture. To encourage open dialogue and lively debate, model how to professionally disagree and accept incomplete ideas. This might feel daring, new or even unsettling for team members. Even if they're experienced, they might not previously have been empowered to work this way. For this reason, you might also want to consider how to stimulate enquiry. This might include making space for under-represented voices to be heard and modelling how to engage with dissenting views in a way that aligns with your school's values.

Finally, build in structured time for reflection to further develop a culture of continuous learning. School leaders and teachers are bombarded by competing priorities and allowing time and space either as individuals or a collective will prove invaluable. When dealing with specific challenges, you might also want to consider how pausing and taking time out to reflect on the evidence base can enable you and the team to make better informed decisions.

### ━━━━━ LINKS TO CLASSROOM PRACTICE 4.1 ━━━━━

Most teams and workplaces will be made up of colleagues with a broad range of experience when it comes to psychological safety, and this won't always be positive.

- What has your experience been? What is your experience now?

Here are some evaluative questions to help you identify what is working well and where you/your setting may need further support.

- If you make a mistake on your team, is it held against you?
- Are you able to bring up problems and tough issues?

- Do people on the team sometimes reject others for being different?
- Is it safe to take a risk?
- Is it difficult to ask other team members for help? Are you able to reflect on why this might be? What role do you/your colleagues play in this?

Naturally how we make sense of our working environments can either set us up for success or prepare us for failure. This is heavily influenced by our decision-making process.

---

## ━━━━━━━ THEORY FOCUS 4.1 ━━━━━━━

### Noticing, Interpreting and Action (Jeong and Brower, 2008)

Theorists Jeong and Brower (2008) examined organisational change and behaviour, the processes by which we make sense of events through three stages.

### Noticing (or Active Thinking)
This is the process by which an individual takes note of an activity or behaviour which interrupts their flow of thinking.

### Interpretation
Through this process an individual uses the data available to them in conjunction with mental models to do one of three things, reaffirm, revise or elaborate on their initial position.

For example, I am a leader carrying out a learning walk in school. I plan to observe my year 5 teacher deliver a literacy lesson. I have seen the teacher deliver a number of strong maths lessons previously and expect this lesson to be strong too. What follows is one of the three outcomes:

- *Reaffirm:* as I anticipated, the literacy lesson is indeed strong.
- *Revise:* the literacy lesson is weaker than I expected, and I have revised my earlier position.
- *Elaborate:* as I anticipated the literacy lesson is strong, but when speaking to the teacher being observed, I discover their background in humanities, and when I talk to the children, I learn that this is their favourite subject. Whilst my earlier mental model provided me with a helpful working hypothesis, the learning walk has provided me with new valuable information.

### Action
The way in which the data has been interpreted will determine the course of action. For example, if the literacy lesson was weak, this will help to inform whether support or further training is required for the teacher.

Day-to-day, teachers and leaders at all levels will want to consider how they can slow down their thinking to make evidence informed decisions. Can you hit pause and ask yourself:

*(Continued)*

- Do I have all the information I need to make an informed decision?
- Am I interpreting fairly?
- What am I missing? What don't I know?

Schools can feel like a pressure cooker. It's all too easy to fall into the trap of making decisions based on emotionally charged conversations, biased data or false perceptions. Considered reflection, informed by teams with cognitive diversity and psychological safety, strengthens evidence-based choices and guards against bias.

---

## THEORY FOCUS 4.2

### Growth Mindset

Psychologist Carol Dweck (2006) introduced the concept of growth mindset – the belief that abilities can be developed through effort and perseverance. This contrasts with a fixed mindset, which assumes abilities are innate and unchangeable.

A growth mindset embraces challenges, persisting through setbacks, seeing effort as a path to mastery, learning from criticism and finding inspiration in the success of others. Unsurprisingly, many advocates of psychological safety (including Amy Edmonson) also champion Growth Mindset since both support learning from failure.

Research shows that pupils with a growth mindset achieve more academically, are more resilient and approach challenges with curiosity. Naturally, these same principles apply to us as adult learners too (Yeager et al., 2019).

Dweck's research concludes that individuals with a fixed mindset are more likely to seek approval, whereas those with a growth mindset are more likely to seek development. Consequently, as educators and leaders, when faced with tough challenges we must ask ourselves (and others), 'Is it that you're not clever enough to solve the problem?... Or is it that you just haven't solved it yet?'

Whilst Dweck's research is not new, it is more important than ever. However, as with all established theories and educational research, we should be mindful of common misconceptions. For example, educators often over emphasise the value of praising effort. Whilst this is an important aspect, we want pupils to put effort into their work so that they may learn to improve. Therefore, praising a pupil who may be putting in lots of effort but is not in fact achieving the learning objective or making progress, will hinder, not help! Effective practice acknowledges effort and provides the learner with specific feedback and a range of strategies they can draw upon. Growth mindset, then, is not about endless effort – it's about effort that leads to learning, improvement and continuous development.

---

## Psychological Safety for Pupils

There are far ranging implications for the psychological safety of pupils in school and beyond the school gates. As educators it's our responsibility to ensure pupils feel included (inclusion safety), able to learn from failure (learner safety), able to contribute (contributor safety) and have the confidence to ask questions and challenge the status quo (challenger safety). We also need to consider systemic barriers to education and potential schools have for reinforcing or upholding these (See Chapter 2 on Belonging).

Naturally, an important part of our role is to prepare pupils for the inevitability of failure; helping children to learn from mistakes and to develop the resilience to pivot when life doesn't go to plan.

A key part of this work involves strengthening executive function (EF). EF refers to a set of skills including, but not limited to, the capacity to plan ahead, meet goals, exercise self-control and stay focused despite distractions. Developing EF skills can help pupils to develop a growth mindset by encouraging them to embrace challenges, persist in the face of setbacks and learn from feedback. With a growth mindset, pupils can develop their cognitive flexibility to help them adapt to changing situations (Tyler, 2022).

## Improving Executive Function Skills

Our genes provide the blueprint for learning EF skills, but they develop through experiences and practice. The foundation is laid in infancy when babies first learn to pay attention. Something as simple as playing a game of peekaboo can help build the early foundations of working memory and self-control as a baby anticipates the surprise.

These skills typically develop most rapidly between ages 3–5, followed by another spike in development during adolescence and early adulthood. As children begin to master EF skills, they're able to successfully navigate more aspects of their environment.

Adults can play an important role in helping children to learn and practice EF skills. Routines, breaking big tasks into small chunks and encouraging games that promote creative thinking, imagination and impulse control. These strategies scaffold the learning for pupils until they can perform them independently.

## Why Executive Function?

Nurturing EF is important if we want children to grow into adults capable of managing competing priorities such as parenting, employment, further education and civic involvement. Competency in EF empowers children to participate more fully in school and prepares them for participation in wider society. Research suggests that when people with strong EF experience poor health, they stick to healthy habits and are more able to effectively manage stress (Diamond, 2013). EF measured in childhood is also an indicator of a range of outcomes including higher socioeconomic status (SES); fewer drug-related problems and criminal convictions in adulthood (Moffitt et al., 2011).

EF skills are malleable, meaning they can change and are influenced by both positive and negative experiences. Stress, poverty and disadvantage can impair impulse control, memory and emotional regulation (Noble et al., 2015). Increased scientific attention has focused on the toxic consequences of stress for brain function and mental and physical health. It's important to note that research is still emerging in this field, but given what we know about the brain's plasticity, evidence suggests that the more a brain does a certain task, the stronger that neural network becomes, making the process more efficient. Repeated practice, combined with supportive caregiving and high-quality early education, can strengthen neural pathways ('cells that fire together, wire together': Posner and Rothbart, 2007) and has the potential to 'repair' the adverse effects of poverty on the developing brain.

## What Does This Mean for Learners?

The EEF toolkit (2025) notes that development of self-regulation and EF is consistently linked with successful learning, including pre-reading skills, early mathematics and problem-solving. Strategies that seek to improve learning by increasing self-regulation have an average impact of eight additional months' progress. However, this is based on very limited evidence in the early years, with a small number of studies having assessed the educational impact of approaches that sought to improve self-regulation.

Childhood EF skills provide an important foundation for all learners. However, it's worth noting, difficulty in mastering EF skills is often associated with several other learning difficulties pupils may face, including neurodevelopmental disorders such as, attention deficit hyperactivity disorder (ADHD) and autism spectrum disorders (ASD). Therefore, strategies for developing pupils EF skills have the potential to help all pupils, including those with protected characteristics.

## ━━━━━━━ CASE STUDY 4.1 ━━━━━━━

### Rathfern Primary School

*This case study is informed by interviews with Naheeda Maharasingam, Headteacher and social justice advocate*

Naheeda Maharasingam, Headteacher of Rathfern Primary School has co-developed an executive function programme with MindSpark CIC, rooted in a strong commitment to equity. The school, an outstanding two-form entry in Lewisham, serves a diverse community.

The leadership team demonstrate their commitment to moral purpose through:

- nurturing powerful self-regulated learners.
- offering a broad and balanced curriculum which promotes a sense of belonging.
- nurturing passionate citizens of the world.

More recently this has included an action research project into the development of the 11 EF skills: metacognition, task initiation, organisation, planning and prioritisation, impulse inhibition, sustained attention, cognitive flexibility, working memory and emotional control.

The leadership team placed a high premium on developing a shared understanding of EF skills from the outset.

Before any work with pupils took place, staff members were asked to assess their own strengths and areas for development against each of the EF skills to determine their EF profile. They explored the idea that an individual's profile may alter in different contexts or when exposed to different stressors. This enabled staff to empathise with pupils who may find certain parts of the school day more challenging, for example break and lunch time, which are traditionally less structured.

The leadership team were also keen that a collegiate approach was adopted. For this reason, the art teacher was commissioned to design an icon for each of the 11 EF skills. Stakeholders, including the pupils, were invited to name the icons. For example, 'Deep thinking Dante' the octopus has three hearts and represents emotional control.

In keeping with this consultative approach, when the team were trained to deliver and roll out EF coaching for pupils, they engaged in 'vertical slicing' to ensure a cross-section of the staff body were included, from midday meal supervisors to class teachers, middle leaders and the Headteacher.

The co-creation of icons, high-quality professional development and high levels of psychological safety resulted in consistency of provision for pupils and fidelity to the programme.

This work was introduced through a multifaceted approach:

- **Foundational Knowledge:** The essential information about EF skills must be learnt so that pupils can then apply this learning in a variety of contexts. For example, key knowledge and language is modelled by the Headteacher in weekly assemblies and rich discussion takes place.
- **Universal offer:** Pupils across all phases are able to take part in weekly EF lessons. In early years this consists of short 10-minute sessions. The time allocated to this increases for each key stage, for example in year 6 pupils take part in sessions lasting 25 minutes.
- **Targeted offer:** When class teachers identify pupils are struggling with a particular executive function, they have the autonomy and agency to deliver an intervention directly related to the EF skill the pupils are struggling with. This may be 'on-the spot' intervention or delivered as pre/post teaching.
- **Intensive coaching:** Identified pupils are also offered 1:1 coaching from a trained EF coach. The sessions last twenty minutes and take place three times a week. The parents of children receiving coaching are also offered high-quality training and meet regularly with coaches to discuss strategies for their child.

Now that this learning is embedded and staff have been able to connect the theory and training to everyday practice, the team have intentionally moved away from a highly structured approach. Instead, they use regular 'teachable' moments throughout the day where pupils can apply their EF skills and knowledge. However, the team has made a conscious choice to keep the systems and processes in place which help to facilitate these conversations, for example pupil 'reflection sheets' with sentence starters and prompts that encourage pupils to reflect on how they could have made a better choice through utilising their EF skills.

Maharasingam explains:

The more time we invest in developing pupil's executive function, the more our school community benefits. This has had policy implications for us; we have re-written our teaching and learning and behaviour policy to reflect our newer way of thinking. We identify and plan opportunities for young people to engage in dialogue, practical tasks and take appropriate actions to become thoughtful, curious, responsible citizens of the planet.

As children move on from the early childhood years and enter primary school, they develop a stronger grasp of their physical world and become more systematic and logical thinkers. Whilst the development of EF skills are beneficial for all pupils, champions of social justice will note intervention

*(Continued)*

disproportionately benefits those with weaker EFs and disadvantaged pupils are more likely to display weaker EFs. As educators we'll want to consider how early EF training can reduce social disparities in achievement and health by reducing the EF gap (Diamond, 2013).

---

### ━━━━━ CASE STUDY 4.2 ━━━━━

## Chance UK

*This case study is informed by interviews with Laura Aznar, Senior Communications and External Affairs Manager*

Chance UK is a small charity with a big heart and enormous reach. Based in London, the charity delivers mentoring programmes for 5–11-year-olds and provides family support across the UK. The benefits of mentoring are highlighted in Chapter 11; however, the work of Chance UK is included here because their person-centred approach to mentoring means that they're uniquely placed to share their practice in developing children's resilience.

Due to circumstances beyond their control, many of the young people who turn to Chance UK for help, struggle to make choices that enable them to achieve their goals. Consequently, this can result in young people making choices that they know the world will view as 'mistakes'. For children already struggling with feelings of low self-esteem this can be overwhelming. Through one-to-one mentoring, group sessions and school workshops, experts at Chance UK support children to develop a growth mind set.

The team understand that progress is not linear. The theme of resilience in the face of adversity runs throughout the organisation and the team model these values. Senior Communications and External Affairs Manager, Laura Aznar explains:

> From the executive team to the frontline youth workers, we are required to be a resilient bunch. We'll do what is necessary to make sure our children, young people and families have the support they need. We might have a detailed plan of support in place, but if it doesn't work, we keep going and try something different. It's become our unofficial motto.

The charity has over 25 years' experience working with children who have faced trauma in their childhood and use evidence-based interventions to respond to each child's individual needs. The seven principles below outline their approach:

1  Child-centred: Support is centred on the needs of the young person/child.
2  Inclusive: Each child and family member are recognised and celebrated as individuals.
3  Holistic: Teams work to understand who a child really is, their unique life experiences and what their physical, mental, emotional and social needs are.
4  Trauma-informed: Teams carry out their work with compassion and sensitivity, respecting that many children have experienced trauma in their lives, and this may manifest itself in different ways.
5  Solution-focused: The charity support children and their families to identify their strengths and use these to build towards their goals.

6 Practical: Experts from Chance UK teach and practice practical skills and techniques that can be used every day to build resilience.

7 Empowering: Youth workers enable children to understand themselves better and to own their own future.

The team are highly collegiate and relentless advocates for pupils and their families. They place a high premium on developing professional relationships with the key individuals in a young person's life, providing supportive challenge where appropriate, to ensure any support is designed with the needs and wants of the young person in mind.

Family engagement is typically very positive. In instances where families have a number of professionals working with them, Chance UK is often the only service they have opted into. Families understand that they're in control and can stop at any time or even request an alternative mentor if they feel the mentor/mentee partnership is not a good match.

Support is currently available to young people through several pathways:

- LIFT Programme: supports girls aged 9–13 who are vulnerable to domestic abuse or have been affected by it. With a strong focus on peer-to-peer support, this programme looks at healthy relationships, consent and building self-confidence.
- Westminster Programme: supports children aged 8–13 who are struggling to manage their emotions or mental health, or who have special educational needs. This programme is designed to build resilience and reduce risk-taking behaviour.
- My Future Programme: supports children aged 5–13 who are struggling to manage their emotions and behaviour, through building self-esteem and self-regulation.
- Safer Space Plus Programme: supports children aged 8–11 to build their self-esteem and raise awareness of domestic abuse.
- STEP Programme: supports children in year 6 or 7 as they move to secondary school, with a focus on emotional well-being and strengthening resilience.

Mentees are invited to define what success looks like for them and experienced youth workers provide bespoke support. Techniques such as cognitive reframing help children to see challenges as opportunities and manage setbacks.

Perhaps one of the charity's most innovative practices is that there are no fixed criteria for access – children simply need a referral. This sets Chance UK apart from many other organisations and support services. They recognise that many of the young people who have accessed their services were unable to receive help anywhere else and some of the young people referred had unmet needs. A critical factor when we consider of the exclusions recorded in 2023/2024, pupils with Education Health and Care Plans (EHCPs) were 3.6 times more likely to be permanently excluded and those on Special Educational Needs (SEN) Support were 5.2 times more likely to be permanently excluded compared to those without SEN (Department of Education, 2025).

Chance UK aims never to turn a child away: mentoring is fully funded; the online referral form is as accessible as possible. Any adult can refer (for example teacher, teaching assistant, parent, friend, neighbour or social worker) – referral forms are swiftly reviewed, and children can be matched with a mentor in less than a week.

(Continued)

The matching exercise is a delicate one. Research indicates that a poorly matched mentor can in fact do more harm than good (Shaw and Bernardes, 2018). Chance UK takes a needs-led approach, considering each child's experiences, strengths and preferences, alongside mentors' specialisms. Whilst it is essential to gain a deepened understanding of the challenges each young person faces; the team of youth workers are mindful not to fall into the trap of viewing the child's life through 'a deficit lens'. Instead, they seek first to understand the whole child, starting with what is going well for that young person and their family.

A typical 1:1 mentoring programme lasts nine months at Chance UK, with approximately three months spent getting to know the child and becoming a trusted adult in the child's life, three months 'doing the work' and providing mentorship and three months preparing the children for transition and a positive ending.

However, as support is needs led, weekly caseload reviews ensure each child has access to bespoke support and this timeframe can be shortened or extended where necessary and where appropriate other pathways and levels of family support are available from light-touch check-ins to intensive family work.

Much of the charity's success lies in drawing upon collaborative, community-led work, bringing stakeholders together to address complex local issues and work towards systemic change.

This place-based support is clearly having tremendous impact and a recent evaluation of the participants that took part in mentoring in 2023 showed 100% of children increased self-esteem, 85% found new friendships and 87% strengthened resilience and behaviour management (Smith and Howard, 2025).

So, what is next for this small but mighty powerhouse? With a new 5-year strategy centred on the theme of Belonging, the charity remains as ambitious as ever for children and young adults. CEO, Vanessa Hall explains:

> We believe that with the right support at the right time, every child can flourish. It is our mission to support children to develop the emotional and social skills they need to thrive in a changing world and to do that, we need to remain child-centred and embrace the diversity of everyone we work with. We are passionate about championing early support that is trans-formative for children and families.

---

## ━━━━━━ LINKS TO CLASSROOM PRACTICE 4.2 ━━━━━━

1  In what ways did the case studies describe developing the grit and resilience of young people?
2  How can support staff, teachers and leaders collaborate to foster a growth mindset? Consider the following:
    ○  Do teams normalise making mistakes and experiencing failure and use personal examples or examples from others?

- Is student effort praised? Are they praised for their use of strategies for learning (metacognition and executive function skills), rather than intelligence?
- Are pupils taught that feedback is an important part of the learning process? Are a range of teaching strategies utilised to scaffold learning?
- Do leaders challenge the idea that learning should feel easy, in order to develop pupils' grit and resilience?
- Do professionals share the view that our abilities can develop and improve over time? Do teachers explicitly explain to pupils that through 'deliberate practice' and regular feedback we are able to get better at the things we struggle with?
- How might we develop these strategies further in our settings?

## Summary

In this chapter, we sought to understand what it really means to fail. We learnt that failure, when reframed, can teach us important lessons and experimentation, within safe parameters, can lead to innovation and growth.

Ideally, we'll be working in settings where psychological safety is the cultural norm and leadership teams develop a culture of 'listening' rather than placing the emphasis on the employee to 'speak up'. Where that isn't our lived reality, we can choose to live out the principles of psychological safety within our zone of influence.

Psychological safety doesn't just help people to 'feel good' or foster a more diverse and inclusive work environment, although it does both of these things. It's a significant factor in team effectiveness, employee retention and enables teams to perform better.

To mitigate risk and minimise mistakes, we want to understand how teams make decisions. We examined theories on sense-making and growth mindset to help leaders understand how colleagues make sense of their working environments and develop resilience. We examined how learners – young and old – benefit from having a range of strategies at their disposal. Case studies showed the benefits of executive function, examining how this can be used as a vehicle for equity. If one of our chief aims is to prepare children for life beyond the school gates, including the ability to manage setbacks, then as educators we're compelled to ask are we meeting the needs of most, or *all* of our pupils? And to what extent?

Ultimately a culture of continuous learning – where we challenge assumptions and learn from mistakes – benefits everybody. Failure can be difficult, but it doesn't need to define us. Reflection, using the strategies discussed in this chapter, enables us to turn errors into stepping stones to success. The most challenging mistakes are the ones we fail to learn from.

**Reflective Task**

Now that you've completed Chapter 4, take a moment to reflect:

1  Can you recall an occasion at work when you felt psychologically safe?
2  What was it about that interaction that enabled you to feel empowered?
3  How did this positively impact the quality of your work? Your interactions with others?
4  List three ways you could further develop psychological safety through interactions with colleagues and pupils.

# References

Department for Education (2025) *Suspensions and permanent exclusions in England, academic year 2023/24*. Available at: https://explore-education-statistics.service.gov.uk/find-statistics/suspensions-and-permanent-exclusions-in-england/2023-24 (Accessed 18 August 2025).

Diamond, A. (2013) 'Executive functions', *Annual Review of Psychology*, *64*(1), pp. 135–168. https://doi.org/10.1146/annurev-psych-113011-143750

Dweck, C. S. (2006) *Mindset: The new psychology of success*. New York: Random House.

Edmonson, A. (2023) *Right kind of wrong*. London Cornerstone Press.

Jeong, H.-S. and Brower, R. S. (2008) 'Extending the present understanding of organizational sensemaking', *Administration & Society*, *40*(3), pp. 223–252. https://doi.org/10.1177/0095399707313446

Moffitt, T. E., Arseneault, L., Belsky, D., Dickson, N., Hancox, R. J., Harrington, H., Houts, R., Poulton, R., Roberts, B. W., Ross, S., Sears, M. R., Thomson, W. M. and Caspi, A. (2011) 'A gradient of childhood self-control predicts health, wealth, and public safety', *Proceedings of National Academy of Science U.S.A.*, *108*(7), pp. 2693–2698. https://doi.org/10.1073/pnas.1010076108

Minnick, J. (2023) *How psychological safety affects employee productivity*. Ragan Communications. Available at: https://www.ragan.com/how-psychological-safety-affects-employee-productivity/ (Accessed 3 January 2025).

Noble, K. G., Houston, S. M., Brito, N. H., Bartsch, H., Kan, E., Kuperman, J. M., Akshoomoff, N., Amaral, D. G., Bloss, C. S., Libiger, O., Schork, N. J., Murray, S. S., Casey, B. J., Chang, L., Ernst, T. M., Frazier, J. A., Gruen, J. R., Kennedy, D. N., Van Zijl, P., Mostofsky, S., [...] Sowell, E. R. (2015) 'Family income, parental education and brain structure in children and adolescents', *Nature Neuroscience*, *18*(5), pp. 773–778. https://doi.org/10.1038/nn.3983

Posner, M. I. and Rothbart, M. K. (2007) 'Research on attention networks as a model for the integration of psychological science', *Annual Review of Psychology*, *58*(1), pp. 1–23. https://doi.org/10.1146/annurev.psych.58.110405.085516

Shaw, B. and Bernardes, E. (2018) *Forging futures through mentoring: A risk worth pursing?* London: Children's Commissioner.

Smith, P. and Howard, S. (2025) *An analysis of the impact of Chance UK's mentoring programme.* London: Chance UK.

The Education Endowment Foundation (EEF). (2025) *Metacognition and self-regulation.* Available at: https://educationendowmentfoundation.org.uk/education-evidence/teaching-learning-toolkit/metacognition-and-self-regulation (Accessed 29 August 2025).

Tyler, R. (2022) *Adopting a growth mindset is key to your success and happiness.* Connections in Mind. Available at: https://connectionsinmind.com/growth-mindset/ (Accessed 3 January 2025).

Yeager, D. S., Hanselman, P., Walton, G. M., Murray, J. S., Crosnoe, R., Muller, C., Tipton, E., Schneider, B., Hulleman, C. S., Hinojosa, C. P., Paunesku, D., Romero, C., Flint, K., Roberts, A., Trott, J., Iachan, R., Buontempo, J., Yang, S. M., Carvalho, C. M., [...] Dweck, C. S. (2019) 'A national experiment reveals where a growth mindset improves achievement', *Nature, 573*, pp. 364–369. Available at: https://www.nature.com/articles/s41586-019-1466-y (Accessed 3 January 2025).

# 5

# Professional Development

---

**Key Terms**

---

These terms may be of use in understanding this chapter and subsequently facilitating discussions with colleagues in your school(s).

**Andragogy** is the study and practice of adult learning.

**Critical Reflection:** Challenging one's own assumptions and beliefs.

**Constructivism** is the idea that learning is an active process of constructing knowledge rather than a passive process of receiving it.

**Didagogy** is the discipline concerned with teaching teachers, focusing on the principles, practices, and conditions needed for effective and meaningful teacher learning and professional development.

---

## Introduction

We've all been there. It's the end of a long day, everyone's exhausted but it's the scheduled weekly staff meeting, the allocated hour for professional development. Competing priorities leave you feeling conflicted. You want to give the trainer your full attention, but find yourself glancing at the clock, waiting for session to end, so that you can get back to the rest of your 'to do' list.

We know that teachers and leaders value professional development in principle. 70% of professionals engage in training to improve their teaching, while 74% of leaders consider teacher development to be important for school improvement purposes (Ofsted, 2024). Research also highlights the far-reaching benefits for both pupils and professionals.

When it comes to professional development, our understanding has developed significantly, and yet all too often, professional development programmes fail to deliver. As recently as 2021, only two-fifths of teachers surveyed described their professional development as effective (Ofsted, 2024).

So how do we continue to upskill as a profession, taking into consideration what we now know about the science of learning and the demands placed upon busy school leaders, teachers and support staff?

This chapter explores research that has informed educational policy and approaches to professional development. We look at the role of psychological safety in creating environments that are conducive to learning and refer to case studies from experts across the sector, inviting you to reflect on how professional development is designed, delivered and evaluated in your setting.

## How Can Research Inform Our Practice?

The Department for Education recently commissioned Ofsted to carry out an independent review of professional development; the review included national surveys and school visits. Their published report (Ofsted, 2024) confirmed that most schools were acutely aware high-quality professional development (PD) can significantly improve pupil outcomes. However, during the pandemic, teacher's access to PD was limited due to staff absence and shortages. During this period, we saw the introduction of online learning for both pupils and staff, though the majority of those surveyed welcomed the return of in-person sessions.

The report explains that teachers expressed a desire for more PD and were keen that leaders consider how PD would be followed up. However senior leaders and experienced teachers explained workload was often a barrier and prevented this from taking place. This was less true for teachers who were new to the profession and typically had protected time to take part in PD.

Most schools have chosen to prioritise training and PD on the curriculum since 2021. This is perhaps no surprise, given Ofsted's recent focus on the quality of education in the inspection framework.

Despite this focus, in approximately half of the schools visited, teachers still had a limited understanding of curriculum design. Time had been spent preparing for inspection, but not necessarily on the mechanics of curriculum development, therefore limiting teacher's understanding.

Practitioners also described a need for more training on teaching pupils with special education needs and/or disabilities (SEND). We know that over time there has been an increase in the number of pupils identified as having SEND. This combined with the shortage of special school provision has resulted in increased pressure being placed on mainstream settings.

Post pandemic there has also been a greater focus on training and development in mental health and well-being for both adults and pupils. Whilst we have seen a decline in the well-being and mental health of young people over time, evidence suggests that this has accelerated since the pandemic, therefore many schools have responded by making adaptations to their provision and professional development offer.

A report from the Education Policy Institute (EPI, 2020) reviewing the effects of high-quality professional development on teachers and pupils, confirms that high-quality training can significantly impact pupil outcomes. A perhaps lesser known fact is that an effective PD programme can significantly close the knowledge gap between new qualified teachers and experienced teachers. In fact, research shows, the impact of great PD on pupil outcomes is similar to having a teacher with 10 years' experience (EPI, 2020).

Interestingly the report also showed that high-quality PD can have similar benefits to that of large structural reforms. In fact, PD has greater effect on pupil attainment than other interventions which school leaders are often encouraged to consider (for example lengthening the school day), and of course, PD initiatives are likely to be well received by teachers and support staff.

There's also encouraging news when it comes to teacher retention, specifically for early career teachers. We know that when teachers do choose to leave the profession, it's usually due to a range of contributing factors, but early data suggests that improved access to training at the start of teachers' careers and access to mentorship have been particularly effective for improving retention rates.

So in the light of the overwhelming evidence that PD can help pupils make significant gains, upskill, improve retention rates and is cost effective; why is it that the majority of training carried out in schools doesn't meet the government's criteria for high quality and how can we resolve this? (EPI, 2021)

# Recommendations

The Education Policy Institute offers a range of recommendations for teachers, school leaders and policy makers on the successful implementation of PD. Recognising that teacher turnover significantly limits impact, they suggest investing in programmes that can offer a degree of flexibility to account for mobility. Whilst this can be difficult to achieve in practice, online and hybrid models can supplement an existing PD offer and provide support for colleagues, including those joining a PD programme part way through the academic year.

The Ambition Institute (Barker, 2020) also identified the drivers for a professional environment that's conducive to learning.

## Start With Purpose

As simple as it might sound, we want to begin by asking ourselves 'What do want teachers and support staff to learn? How can we support them to achieve this? How are staff supported with the daily challenges they face?'

PD will be considerably more impactful if staff understand how the persistent problems they face relate to the school's development plan. Then they need to be supported to develop the specialised expertise required to tackle the issue at hand.

## Create the Right Conditions for Development to Take Place

A trusting work environment is integral to the success of the individual and team. Therefore, school culture has an important role to play. Employees want to know they're being invested in, but they'll also want to be seen, valued and understand that their contribution matters.

## Draw Upon What We Know About How Humans Learn

Teachers and support staff are susceptible to all the same challenges that pupils face, distractions and lack of motivation – to name a few. Fortunately, as a profession we are much better informed now about the science of learning, we plan for retrieval practice and spaced learning because we know it supports knowledge retention. Leaders will want to consider how they incorporate the same principles for effective teaching that are used for pupils (clear modelling, feedback on progress) and apply this to adult learning.

Incorporate mechanisms which evidence suggests is likely to lead to habit change.

When PD is less successful, it's delivered in way that doesn't result in a change in behaviour. Therefore, staff might appear engaged during the session, but the practice 'on the ground' doesn't change and therefore the pupil experience doesn't alter. Leaders will want to refer to evidence informed practice which facilitates change (See the Education Endowment Fund's 2021 guidance on professional development).

## Be Prepared to Commit Time, Energy and Resource

New concepts need to be revisited over time. Leaders will want to consider how PD is followed up, how to motivate staff and how to positively acknowledge progress. Changes in behaviour take time and this will also need to be planned for.

# The Role of Psychological Safety

If we're serious about creating the right conditions for learning, then it's impossible to ignore the role of psychological safety. What was once seen as 'nice to have' is now recognised as integral by high performing teams across industries.

There are several key factors to consider here, including the learner's need to feel respected, the structure of the training and the learner's readiness to learn.

When leaders invest in fostering a supportive environment, one where employee's feel comfortable taking risks, making mistakes and asking for help, it results in increased engagement. A psychologically safe environment that encourages open and honest communication facilitates innovation.

## How Do We Know If We're Getting It Right?

Professional development has been notoriously difficult for schools to evaluate effectively, but with dwindling school budgets, it's more important than ever that school leaders are able to rationalise their choices and demonstrate impact over time. Guskey's model for evaluating professional development (2000) provides teachers and leaders with a framework for doing exactly this.

He suggests the following five aspects are reviewed:

1 Participants' reactions: This is typically where evaluation usually starts and stops in schools. A simple overview (usually an online survey) which seeks to capture whether participants enjoyed the session and determine how useful or engaging they found the session. This often includes questions about how knowledgeable the facilitator was and opportunities to suggest improvements.

2 Participants' learning: This is your opportunity to find out whether colleagues have acquired the intended knowledge and skills from the training that was delivered. Schools will need to choose which mechanism/platform they want to use to capture this. What's right for one school may look very different from another school. This will be informed by each setting's vision, values, culture and several other variables, for example where you are in your own school improvement journey. Evaluation of participant's learning might be something you ask colleagues to reflect on themselves, something that's addressed in scheduled line management meetings, or discussed in staff briefings with the wider team. Leaders will also want to consider how this information is tracked over time; ideally sharing this data with stakeholders to inform and shape future PD offers.

3 Review of implementation: Here teams are encouraged to look at the impact on the wider school and the way the leadership team have supported the implementation of any new learning. For example, how has new learning been embedded through processes and policies? Did teachers and support staff receive sufficient support to meaningfully implement the new strategy or skills asked of them? Has enough time been allocated? Teams might choose to evaluate this through their school development plans, through dedicated time in staff meetings or existing platforms for staff feedback.

4 Participants use of knowledge and skills: This is the team's opportunity to gain a deeper understanding of how new knowledge and skills are being applied. This will also help leadership teams to understand how effective implementation has been. To gain the most from this exercise, leaders will want to triangulate information from a range of sources this might include, low-stakes learning walks, drop-ins, teacher self-reflection, peer-observations and line management meetings.

5 Student learning outcomes: Of course, what all stakeholders really want to know is what was the impact on pupils? Consider what specifically you want to measure here and why? Are the desired outcomes seen through attainment and progress data or attendance data? Perhaps they're behavioural or attitudinal? Be intentional about how this will be collated from the outset, to gather the most accurate evidence base. For example, you may want to consider using both quantitative data (pupil exam results, attendance data) and qualitative data (pupil and parent surveys).

Guskey describes the need for all five aspects to be reviewed, as each aspect is interconnected and builds on the one before. He reminds us that this framework is intended to be used to evaluate impact but can also be used to plan for meaningful, high-quality PD.

## ━━━━━━━━━ LINKS TO CLASSROOM PRACTICE 5.1 ━━━━━━━━━

Consider Guskey's model of evaluation (2000).

How are the following five aspects evaluated with rigour in your setting? Which aspects might benefit from further development?

- Participant's reaction
- Participant's learning
- Organisation and support
- Participant's use of knowledge and skills
- Pupils' learning outcomes

How could a combination of both quantitative data and qualitative data inform the evaluation process?

## ━━━━━━━━━ CASE STUDY 5.1 ━━━━━━━━━

## The Reach Foundation

*This case study is informed by interviews with Jon Hutchinson, Director of Curriculum and Teacher Development, international Fellow with New America, and cofounder of Meno Academy.*

In addition to his numerous other projects, Jon Hutchinson was recently part of the government's independent Curriculum and Assessment Review panel. He believes as a profession, we've come a long way. This is reflected in the large number of practitioners that travel from around the globe to learn more about our delivery and approach.

> In particular, we've made significant progress in the last 15 years, with increasing numbers of schools and school leaders recognising that professional development should be rooted in an evidence base rather than the direction of travel being driven by the strongest personality or most charismatic leader. As a result, we're now well placed to have rich conversations about how evidence translates to the classroom.

> Of course, there have been missteps over time, for example instances when the application of evidence into practice is too generalised and doesn't take into consideration contextual barriers, but we're slowly and surely getting better at this too.

Jon explains nationally many more schools and school leaders are recognising the true value of professional development. Since approximately 2014, there has been a growing consensus that professional development should be sustained over time, a shift from the outdated piecemeal, 'pick and mix' approach, where leaders might plan 39 staff meeting sessions across the academic year, each on a different theme – for example, a session on concrete resources in maths followed by one on vocabulary – often with little thought as to how this learning might be followed up. Yet, we know from our own experiences of learning – whether that's learning the guitar or a new language – that taught content needs careful sequencing. It's pleasing to see increasing numbers of schools adopting spaced learning and interweaving, making learning stick for adults as we do for pupils.

Of course, there are times when a 'one off' session is appropriate. For example, if school leaders choose to introduce greeting each pupil at the classroom door as part of well-established practices on self-regulation, this may not warrant a series of professional development meetings.

More typically, schools introduce broad initiatives that require careful sequencing and planning over time.

Jon specifically warns of the 'jingle fallacy,' where a single term is used to describe multiple approaches. 'Coaching' is a prime example of this.

The term coaching is increasingly used to describe a school's approach to improving teacher performance; however, the term is used liberally and often without consensus or a shared understanding of what we mean when refer to 'coaching' or how this is carried out at classroom level.

At Reach there is a fairly directive approach to instructive coaching: feedback typically narrates what was observed, the resulting knowledge gap and the skill needed to close it, followed by guided practice.

Jon recognises that a directive approach isn't necessarily for everyone. The team at Reach recruit staff who are receptive to this approach and hire with this quality in mind. This creates a strong culture over time, as employees understand at the point of interview, if I'm joining the school, directive instructional coaching is part of the school and trust's culture. Strong cultures aren't built overnight. Jon stresses the importance of knowing your people, understanding the context and history of the school and moderating professional development approaches accordingly. Noting, that this also relates to the level of collaboration expected. He points to examples of school cultures where teams previously carried out high-stakes lesson observations at three points in the year and subsequently introduced support plans where these individuals did not meet expectations. When these same teams are rapidly introduced to a model of instructional coaching and informed overnight that 'drop-ins' will take place once a week, we can inadvertently make low-stakes activities feel high-stakes, generating resistance or reluctance to engage. Therefore, knowing your people and understanding the context and history of the school is key when considering how new strategies are implemented.

Things are changing. We've already seen a culture shift with the introduction of the Early Careers Framework model. All new teachers qualifying to teach will now be familiar with deliberate practice. This has taken place in conjunction with the introduction of low-stakes learning walks and lesson 'drop-ins', now that most schools have moved away from graded lesson observations. Naturally some practitioners will be more familiar with these than others, and they'll take time to embed.

As a result of these cumulative changes, we're now able to envisage a point in the near future where it will become the cultural norm for teachers to view high-quality PD as their entitlement and spend dedicated time developing mental models. When we see professional development implemented less successfully, practice reverts to traditional approaches – 'this is how I do it, now you do it this way too'.

Jon explains this inadvertently caps the teacher's ability to employ adaptive teaching techniques which are integral to ensuring our classrooms are equitable.

*(Continued)*

Alternative approaches to feedback can foster adaptive teaching techniques. This might involve a deeper reflection and rather than narrating the knowledge gap that was created, engaging the teacher in a two-way professional dialogue, enquiring 'What was the intended outcome of the learning objective and activity? How else could you have achieved that? Where could you use that strategy? Where wouldn't you use that strategy?'

Whilst this approach is less directive, over time, it empowers the teacher to develop their 'teaching toolkit' over time.

Jon also stresses the importance of consciously creating the right conditions for professional development so that the new strategy or initiative being launched can take root. He works with teams to explore how strong cultures are created and underpinned by a sense of belonging. He explains, school leaders should be wary of assuming 'buy-in' to a new strategy is unidirectional.

As school leaders it's easy to assume that when we get the 'buy-in', a strategy will be successful. If we're not careful, this can lead to delayed implementation (due to a lack of support for the initiative) or patchy implementation. Instead of insisting on wholesale, large-scale change, when implementing new initiatives, consider focusing on the 'small wins'. Sharing team successes early on in implementation encourages the team to move on the next small achievable goal.

Jon cites uniform as an example. When looking to implement changes or make improvements we can set unrealistic expectations, then become deflated when these are not realised. What if rather than tackling uniform in its entirety, the whole team focused their energy on encouraging pupils to do up their top button? Zeroing in on that one small micro step to success. Then, once we see progress with this aspect of implementation, in line with EEF guidance (2021), we celebrate and acknowledge the success, with emphasis on the collaborative effort of the team to capitalise on good will and momentum; 'We did it! Now what do we want to focus on next?'

Naturally, the emotional and cognitive aspects of 'buy-in' are vital to sustaining culture and embedding professional development or new strategy. Leaders need to be able to communicate their 'why'. However, if what the teacher is subsequently asked to implement is unclear, feels overwhelming or appears nonsensical, then this undermines the rationale. It will also undermine any attempt to create a psychologically safe environment that is conducive to innovation.

Finally, to secure 'buy-in', allow plenty of time for teachers to translate the theory and research they have received through professional development into classroom practice. Schedule dedicated time for practitioners to consider how new initiatives might be implemented in the classroom and acknowledge in-house expertise. For example, when delivering professional development on retrieval, as a leader you'll want to be clear on how and why retrieval works and the evidence base to support this, but there's still scope to acknowledge that the key stage 4 art teacher is best placed to translate how these principles are applied to their specific subject domain. This ensures staff expertise is acknowledged, and team members feel seen and heard. This approach also fosters a culture of mutual accountability as teachers, alongside leaders, are empowered and trusted to implement change.

# CASE STUDY 5.2

## Steplab

*This case study is informed by interviews with Rachel Sewell, Director of Implementation, former English teacher and Vice Principal and Ania Townsend, Director of Communities former History teacher, ITT curriculum subject leader and Senior Leader in London Secondary schools.*

Rachel Sewell and Ania Townsend shared their thinking on Steplab's forthcoming implementation road map, emphasising that improvement initiatives are prone to failure when one person is tasked with heralding the professional development offer. When leaders embark on a new initiative, without first uniting the team they're simply less likely to be successful. For this reason, the team at Steplab have been supporting leaders to build a sense of community and develop a shared understanding of how learning happens.

The team are particularly interested in how training and professional development takes place within school settings and the interplay between professional development and school culture. Specifically, the way in which leaders ensure there is alignment of vision and how this vision is shared, as this will determine how much support there is for the strategy or initiative that is being introduced.

Josh Goodrich CEO and co-founder of Steplab, asks us to consider the analogy of oarsman rowing in sync; the progress made and trajectory of travel when everyone is pulling together versus the lack of progress when team members are rowing in different directions. We know that when individuals are busy promoting their own initiatives (however well intended), rather than collectively working towards shared school priorities, this can negatively impact pupil progress and attainment.

Josh refers to the four pillars of implementation, which include:

1 Culture: The team at Steplab deliver professional development internationally. It quickly became clear that supporting leaders to build a positive feedback culture in schools was integral to successful implementation. This culture is developed over time through creating an 'open door' approach, ensuring visitors to the classroom are welcomed. As a result, teachers are eager to improve their practice.

2 Training: Leaders will also want to ensure everyone who has responsibility for training receives high-quality PD themselves. This is important for developing a sense of community and raising the profile of professional development in your setting. It will also support teams to establish a shared vocabulary. Codifying your approach will ensure consistency and help to promote a shared understanding.

3 Systems: Leaders that promote and protect psychological safety, keep systems under regular review. Have teachers got time built into their day for professional development? Is this time protected and is it a priority? Leaders who place a high premium on professional development raise its profile within school, benefitting both staff and pupils.

4 Responsive leadership: The team at Step lab have been supporting leaders with how to respond to data, advising leaders on how triangulation of data analysis can inform the provision, supporting leaders to review lesson drop-ins, make micro adjustments and evaluate the impact of instructional coaching.

*(Continued)*

Ania and Rachel are quick to point out that the four pillars of implementation are like a treadmill, they never really finish, because, of course, school improvement never really ends and is cyclical in nature.

Steplab have carried out comprehensive work, encouraging leaders to think deeply about how professional development and training is sequenced. Ours is a profession with many competing priorities. How do we make sure leaders are not pulled in too many different directions? The skill here is to 'make the main thing, the main thing'. Naturally, this is easier said than done. Steplab continue to collaborate tirelessly with leaders to provide teams with practical tools and strategies to achieve exactly this. Recognising that transformational change is achieved through unification, the team explicitly discuss the need to devise systems and structures which facilitate sustainable professional development. They explore the connection between pedagogy and school improvement underpinned by a strong culture and a sense of belonging.

## ━━━━━━ LINKS TO CLASSROOM PRACTICE 5.2 ━━━━━━

Both case studies emphasise the importance of creating the right 'conditions for learning'.

They reference the value of developing a shared language and acknowledge the role that school culture plays.

1  What practical steps can you take to create the right 'conditions for learning' in your setting?
2  What meaningful action could be taken to ensure the team are collectively working towards shared school priorities?

## ━━━━━━ THEORY FOCUS 5.1 ━━━━━━

## Adult Education Theory

Adult Education theory describes adult learning as self-directed and goal-oriented. It acknowledges that all adults have their own unique set of characteristics and bring a wealth of life experience to training sessions. These experiences can be leveraged to enhance learning, but it's important to be aware that they also influence the conditions for effective learning.

Whilst younger learners are still imagining their future selves, adults are already living out this reality and juggling competing priorities. Therefore, they're keen to understand how training will meet their professional or personal needs before committing time and resource.

Adults are more likely to engage in learning when they can understand the purpose and appreciate the value. They express preference for learning that can be immediately applied or training that's directly relevant to their professional lives. Readiness to learn is also acknowledged as an important factor and it's recognised that adults are most motivated to learn when they have a specific need or challenge that they need to overcome or address (Njenga, 2022).

## ━━━━━ THEORY FOCUS 5.2 ━━━━━

### Rational Choice Theory

Rational choice theory also describes learning as a goal-oriented process. However, it takes into consideration how beliefs, interests and opportunities influence decision-making.

The theory works on the premise that people are, for most part, rational creatures who make considered choices once they have assessed the potential outcomes. It assumes that people are generally motivated by self-interest and aim to gain the most from each situation or circumstance.

It describes the decision-making process individuals go through, calculating the cost–benefit analysis each time, evaluating the personal cost to them and weighing this up against the potential benefit, before landing on the outcome which will result in most personal gain.

So, what does this mean for professional development? Well, when we consider teachers as adult learners who are goal-oriented and rational, the implication is that teachers are self-aware and discerning. Teachers are therefore often aware of what knowledge and competencies they need to develop and that awareness guides them in choosing the content they need to learn, and the methods most appropriate to them.

Additionally, they're aware of their context and their ability to deal with the challenges that they must face as part of their professional development. In this instance, PD models which have been co-designed and co-constructed have the potential to be particularly impactful.

---

# Summary

The evidence base tells us that high-quality PD can have a transformative impact on pupil attainment, in addition to having numerous benefits for the workforce and wider profession.

This chapter explored research on how to design and deliver effective professional development. We considered how PD can be evaluated in a robust way that supports planning and delivery.

Psychological safety fundamentally impacts how adults engage with professional development. The absence of psychological safety activates the sympathetic nervous system, increases cortisol production and inevitably clouds our thinking. When learners don't feel psychologically safe, it negatively affects their memory and social skills. However, when we feel comfortable, respected and supported, we're able to make deeper connections and develop new skills more effectively.

Schools that place a high premium on psychological safety, model the kind of supportive culture that encourages personal and professional growth, unlocks innovation and drives school improvement.

— **Reflective Task** —

Now that you've completed Chapter 5, take a moment to reflect.

What practical steps can we take to ensure our PD is as impactful as possible? As a team how can you plan for the following?

- Positive communication patterns (during the session and following on from the PD).
- Ensuring adults know that their voice and their contribution matters.
- An evidenced informed approach to PD.
- The mechanisms you want to use to facilitate professional learning. What do we want to include and why?
- Activities that encourage adults to share their experiences. This validates prior knowledge, and it also strengthens the team. We know that what is assumed or prior knowledge for one learner, might be new learning for another.
- Collaboration. Adults learn and achieve well when working together towards a shared purpose or vision. How do we provide these opportunities for teams?
- Psychological safety. Emotional intelligence is key, for both the facilitator and participants. Are the conditions for learning appropriate? How have we assessed readiness to learn? How will PD be followed up? How can this be further developed and inform policy and practice?

# References

Barker, J. (2020) *Designing effective professional development*. Ambition Institute. Available at: https://www.ambition.org.uk/blog/designing-effective-professional-development/ (Accessed 11 April 2025).

Education Policy Institute (EPI). (2020) *Evidence review: The effects of high-quality professional development on teachers and students*. Available at: https://epi.org.uk/publications-and-research/effects-high-quality-professional-development/ (Accessed 11 April 2025).

Education Policy Institute (EPI). (2021) *The cost of high-quality professional development for teachers in England*. Available at: https://epi.org.uk/publications-and-research/the-cost-of-high-quality-professional-developmentfor-teachers/ (Accessed 11 April 2025).

Guskey, T. R. (2000) *Evaluating professional development*. Thousand Oaks, CA: Corwin Press.

Njenga, M. (2022) 'Teacher participation in continuing professional development: A theoretical framework', *Journal of Adult and Continuing Education*, 29(1), pp. 69–85. https://doi.org/10.1177/14779714221123603

Ofsted (2024) *Independent review of teachers' professional development in schools: Phase 1 findings*. Available at: https://www.gov.uk/government/publications/teachers-professional-development-in-schools/independent-review-of-teachers-professional-development-in-schools-phase-1-findings (Accessed 29 August 2025).

The Education Endowment Foundation (EEF) (2021) *Effective professional development*. Available at: https://educationendowmentfoundation.org.uk/education-evidence/guidance-reports/effective-professional-development (Accessed 11 April 2025).

# 6

# Coaching and Mentoring

## Key Terms

These terms may be of use in understanding this chapter and subsequently facilitating discussions with colleagues in your school(s).

**Mentoring** helps individuals gain valuable insights and advice. It's usually a long-term, ongoing relationship between a mentor and mentee, focused on the mentee's overall personal and professional development. Mentors provide guidance, support and encouragement based on their own experiences and expertise.

**Coaching** is more of a structured, goal-oriented process; coaches help individuals to develop specific skills or improve performance in a particular area. The coach guides and supports the coachee. The process typically lasts for a defined period.

**A sponsor** is a senior leader or influential individual within an organisation who actively advocates for an individual's career advancement.

**Person-centred support** is a care approach that focuses on the needs and preferences of the individual.

**Place-based support** is a holistic approach that considers the needs of a community and the place where people live, work and spend their time. It involves understanding the local context and using that knowledge to coordinate action and investment to improve the quality of life for the community.

## Introduction

Whether you're at the beginning of your teaching career, or an experienced executive, there are numerous benefits to being coached or mentored. It's a process that encourages self-reflection. As a mentor or coach, holding professional space for a colleague is empowering, it enables you to develop your skill set too.

Individuals in positions of power or influence can also accelerate your learning and development through professional dialogue or sponsorship.

Increasing numbers of teachers and leaders are now engaging with models of coaching and mentorship to further develop their skills and competencies within a strong culture of psychological safety.

This chapter explores the theory and research underpinning these approaches; we'll look at examples of innovative practice that enable leaders to learn from newer or less experienced colleagues through peer coaching and reverse mentoring and consider how this adds value to the workforce.

Of course, adults are not the only beneficiaries and in recent years the sector has become increasingly reliant upon mentors and coaches to support our pupils, particularly those who are vulnerable or most at risk. In this chapter, we'll examine a series of case studies to deepen our understanding of highly effective practice for pupils and consider how this might be applied to our own setting.

## How Can Research Inform Our Practice?

Although coaching and mentoring is growing in popularity across schools and colleges, there is still much to learn from the private sector, where 84% of Fortune 500 companies have engaged with mentoring programmes (Cantalupo, 2022). Coaching can support individuals to identify and define their goals, promoting retention and growth. In fact, 25% of employees who enrolled in a mentoring programme experienced an increase in salary, compared to 5% of workers who didn't participate (Sexton, 2023).

As well as benefitting from professional growth, colleagues who engage in mentoring are more likely to believe their colleagues value their work (Wronski, 2019). Mentees across industries also report higher levels of engagement, increased confidence and improved performance (Boulton, 2024).

The dynamic between mentor and mentee allows for personal growth too. This may include a range of soft skills: improved self-awareness, time management or the ability to manage difficult and challenging conversations with colleagues.

Given the numerous benefits it's important to acknowledge who stands to gain the most from these arrangements. We know that globally, women are severely underrepresented in leadership. Nearly seven in ten primary and five and ten secondary school teachers are female, yet we continue to see a lack of representation within school leadership (Bergmann et al. 2022).

Traditionally, career progression has been a leaky pipeline for women. Comprehensive mentoring programmes present an opportunity to change that narrative and 'throw down the ladder' to help the next generation progress.

Whilst we're very slowly becoming a more diverse workforce, there's an urgent need to develop the pipeline for leaders of Global Majority Heritage (Worth et al., 2022) and we must also acknowledge the complexity of intersectionality. For example, when race intersects with gender, pathways to success are narrowed.

In this instance reverse mentoring can be a particularly powerful tool. This is an opportunity to 'flip the script' on traditional mentoring methods and invite less experienced members of the team who happen to be of Global Majority Heritage (GMH), to be paired with more experienced members of the senior leadership team. The most effective mentoring partnerships move beyond 'directive' discussions and become a two-way exchange. Through reverse mentoring GMH team members are empowered to share their knowledge with senior leaders, gain access to professional networks and receive expert advice.

School settings will want to carefully consider how these partnerships are established and how they fit into a wider strategy on Equality, Diversity and Inclusion. A strategic approach will enable leadership teams to measure progress over time. For example, a school may choose to develop leadership pathways for aspiring Black female leaders, as part of a wider plan to develop diversity of thought.

As a sector, we're acutely aware of the social mobility gap. Our pupils' chance of success in life is intrinsically linked to their socio-economic status and parentage. We also know that our own experiences as children follow us into adulthood. Coaching and mentoring programmes present us with a phenomenal opportunity to disrupt negative thought patterns. We're invited to challenge societal norms and the limitations we unwittingly place on ourselves or others. This is crucially important when we consider mentees are five times more likely to be promoted than those without mentors (Sexton, 2023).

It's worth noting the benefits of coaching and mentoring are not limited to the mentee, or the mentor but rather they're multi-faceted and far-reaching. But what exactly does mentoring, coaching and sponsorship involve and why choose one approach over another?

## Mentoring

Mentoring helps individuals gain valuable insights and advice, leading to increased self-awareness, personal growth and career development. It's usually a long-term, ongoing relationship between a mentor and mentee, focused on the mentee's overall personal and professional development. Mentors provide guidance, support and encouragement based on their own experiences and expertise. This is typically (though not always) an experienced colleague who is sharing their knowledge to support the development of a less inexperienced individual. It calls on the skills of questioning, listening, clarifying and reframing that are associated with coaching. Mentoring is typically less structured than coaching, with meetings scheduled as needed and conversations covering a wide range of topics.

## Coaching

Coaching is more of a structured, goal-oriented process; coaches help individuals to develop specific skills or improve performance in a particular area. The coach is typically an expert in the relevant field and uses their experience to guide and support the coachee. The process typically lasts for a defined period or forms the basis of an ongoing management style. Whilst definitions of coaching vary, there are some agreed principles.

Coaching is usually a non-directive form of development focusing on improving performance and developing an individual. Personal factors may be included but the emphasis is on performance at work.

Coaching activities often have both organisational and individual goals, for individuals to assess their strengths and areas for development. It's worth noting that coaching is a highly skilled activity and one which is best delivered by those who are trained and hold a formal qualification. The process is usually time-bound and goal-oriented. Coaching relationships are usually short-term, with specific, measurable goals. They're focused on specific skills and performance improvement and coachees often benefit from formal structure and accountability. This often includes regular, structured meetings with clear expectations and an agreed method for tracking progress.

## Sponsor

Sponsors can influence and have decision-making power. They're senior leaders or influential individuals who actively advocate for a colleague's career advancement. They use their influence and decision-making power to help colleagues gain visibility and access to opportunities. They actively promote other's achievements and potential. A sponsor is also able to focus on visibility and seek out opportunities within, or beyond the organisation, they help colleagues gain exposure to decision-makers and secure promotions or high-profile projects. Their support enables others to gain access to career-advancing opportunities and positions them for long-term success within their setting or sector.

## ━━━━━ CASE STUDY 6.1 ━━━━━

### Aspiring Heads

*This case study is informed by interviews with Nadine and Ethan Bernard, Founder/CEO and Managing Director of Aspiring Heads, a social enterprise dedicated to breaking down racial barriers to education in the UK.*

Aspiring Heads works to increase the representation of Black teachers and educators in school leadership, ultimately creating a more inclusive learning environment for all children. In addition to her role as Founder and CEO, Nadine leads a thriving primary school in South London. Her path to headship, however, was far from easy. It was her personal and professional lived experiences that inspired the creation of Aspiring Heads and continue to shape its mission today. She explains '*I wanted to make sure the next generation of Black educators were better equipped than me. I wanted to give them a better toolkit, so that they're more readily prepared to tackle the challenges that lie ahead*'.

At the peak of the pandemic and shortly after the birth of their third child, Nadine recalls sitting in the kitchen at home with husband, Ethan, reflecting on the staggering low representation of Black headteachers nationally. This was a conversation that was set against the backdrop of the murder of George Floyd and the emergence of the Black Lives Matters movement.

Nadine also reflected on her own lived experience of the education system, both as a child and as a professional. While she recalls positive experiences and memories, there were also deeply traumatic experiences underpinned by the structural racism that still plagues us today.

She explains, *'There were numerous situations where I knew that as a young Black female, my value and worth and whether or not I had anything to contribute, had already been decided before I had even opened my mouth. If you're denied opportunities or de-valued often enough, it will of course affect your self-esteem'.*

All her experiences, positive and negative, have informed how Nadine chooses to lead today, with compassion, high expectations and a person-centred approach. Her vision is deeply rooted in psychological safety. Nadine is keen to impress upon the team that mistakes are learning opportunities, and a culture of supportive challenge is encouraged. Challenging traditional power structures is something Nadine has significant experience of, and she's happy to share these experiences with course participants from Aspiring Heads. She explains *'I want aspiring leaders to learn how to navigate the challenges of leadership and to be able to do so in a safe space. A space where they can show up as themselves. A space where they belong'.*

Winners of the Fair Education Alliance award in 2021, Aspiring Heads offer a six-month online programme with access to podcasts, a reflection workbook and online modules covering far ranging topics including how to become values driven and develop resilience. These modules are reinforced with the latest research and evidence and supported by a range of experts in the field including Paul Miller Professor of Educational Leadership and Social Justice and Director of the Institute for Educational and Social Equity. Coaching and mentoring are also key features of the course. Nadine describes this process from her perspective, *'What I enjoy most is being able to offer aspiring leaders the time and space to reflect, because you know deep down, they have the answers themselves. You're just there to help bring it to the surface. It's a joy to watch them grow and develop'.*

To date Aspiring Heads have mentored eight cohorts and one in three participants have stepped into leadership roles or subsequently received promotions during their time on the programme. Course participants affectionately describe the programme as 'joining the AH family'. Throughout the process they form a trusted community. In recognition of this, participants can elect to become part of the AH alumni upon completing the course, which grants them access to additional resources, events and networking opportunities designed to further support their leadership journey, including ad hoc support from the CEO and Managing Director.

# The Importance of a Strong Start

While it's possible to benefit from coaching and mentoring at any stage in our career, it's essential that teachers joining the profession enjoy a positive experience. So, what are the key ingredients that set Early Career Teachers up for success?

## High-Quality Mentorship

Effective mentors are knowledgeable and highly skilled communicators. They create a safe space to have honest conversations and provide candid feedback. They are generous in sharing their expertise and draw upon a range of strategies such as co-planning, modelling, rehearsing, networking and collaboration. They enable the mentee to feel supported and learn through reflection.

The National Institute of Teaching's report on the mentoring and coaching of teachers (2023) also points to the importance of effective mentor training. The study suggests that when individuals volunteer to take part in mentoring or when pairings take place in the same key stage or within similar areas of expertise, they're more likely to result in successful partnerships.

School leaders will also want to consider practical limitations to ensure smooth delivery and to ensure sufficient resource is allocated. Whilst the introduction of virtual meetings has led to increased flexibility, it might be useful to think about the logistics of timetabling and agreed meeting spaces. How close in proximity are mentoring part- nerships? Will this enable pairings to develop a close rapport? How can any practical challenges be overcome?

To promote and drive a culture where a high premium is placed on mentoring, you may want to look at how this is prioritised within the setting. Are mentors able to access high quality training? How is their contribution celebrated and acknowledged? How is feedback from mentors and mentees gathered and triangulated to ensure a shared understanding is developed?

The report also confirms that non-evaluative mentoring can result in increased trust and open communication between the mentor and mentee. Therefore, ideally teacher appraisal will be completely independent of any mentoring processes to ensure maximum impact. When a mentor also assumes responsibility for line management, this can limit effectiveness.

## How Do I Find a Mentor, Coach and Sponsor?

Aspiring and established leaders can source accredited mentors or coaches. This is an excellent way to work with trained professionals with a proven track record. There are also increasing numbers of national bodies and professional networks that can offer support (such as The National Institute of Teaching).

Seek out a colleague at work. Is there someone in your team or perhaps another local school with a particular skill set or knowledge base that you can learn from? Consider writing a carefully crafted email to this person. Be clear about your intentions and explain why you would specifically like to work with them. If directly approaching the individual feels too daunting, try contacting their line manager, again stating your intention and politely requesting an introduction.

Who has left an impression on you throughout your teaching career? Are there any past connections that you've developed a rapport with who may be a supportive coach or mentor at this stage in your career?

Often the most effective partnerships are developed with colleagues who are no longer employees at the same organisation and therefore no longer have 'skin in the game'. These individuals are able to bring a fresh perspective and a sense of objectivity.

Put the word out. Join professional networking groups and use social media platforms as a vehicle to widen your reach.

## ━━━━━ THEORY FOCUS 6.1 ━━━━━

### GROW Model

The GROW model, developed by Sir John Whitmore and colleagues in the late 1980s, has since gained widespread adoption by the private and public sector in numerous countries. More recently it has also been included in National Professional Qualification Headship (NPQH) training materials.

GROW is an acronym outlining four key stages of a coaching conversation:

- Goal: Define what needs to change moving forward. Coach and coachee agree on a clear, measurable objective and set the tone for discussion.
- Reality: Reflect on the current situation. The coachee describes their context, while the coach gently challenges assumptions, asks clarifying questions and builds understanding.
- Options: Explore possible ways forward. The coach can get creative, offer suggestions mindfully and use probing questions to unlock fresh perspectives that enable the person being coached to move forward.
- Will: Commit to next steps. Consider challenges, timelines and required support. Discuss how to mitigate risk and what professional development will be required to ensure action is realistic and achievable.

Of course, as with any coaching model there are both advantages and limitations to this model. On the one hand the model allows the coachee to take responsibility whilst also being supported throughout the process.

However, its effectiveness depends on setting realistic goals. If the coach is not based in the same workplace or setting, then naturally they will not be aware of the challenges 'on the ground' and will, to some extent, be reliant on the coachee recognising these through reflective questioning.

## ━━━━━ LINKS TO CLASSROOM PRACTICE 6.1 ━━━━━

- What steps can we take to ensure the delivery of coaching and mentoring is high quality and results in high impact?
- How can we work with the mentees and mentors in our provision to ensure a shared vision and understanding of mentoring are established?

## Mentoring for Pupils and Young Adults

As a sector, we continue to see growing numbers of pupils' struggle with the daily challenges of school. This is set against a backdrop of stark statistics on school absence and increasing numbers of pupils struggling with mental health. As a result, more and more schools have turned to mentoring to ensure pupils are equipped to navigate school and life beyond the school gates.

There is a mixed evidence base when it comes to the implementation of mentoring for children. This is in part due to studies measuring a variety of different performance indicators and due to the mechanisms, which need to be in place for mentoring to be a 'success'.

The evidence base is still developing, and the Education Endowment Fund (2025) report that the impact of mentoring varies but, on average, leaders can expect a positive impact on attainment. Pupils in receipt of mentor typically make up to two months additional progress.

The Children's Commissioner's report on mentoring (Shaw and Bernardes, 2018), also reveals a modest positive effect (with clearer benefit to academic outcomes than social and emotional outcomes). However, it is worth exercising caution here, due to the relatively low number of studies in this area. The study does confirm though, that mentoring is more beneficial for young people from disadvantaged backgrounds. We also know that successful mentoring pairings for children are contingent on:

- Preparing both mentors and mentees beforehand through training, guidance and ensuring clear expectations are established.
- Taking a flexible approach. Ensuring the process is 'child-centred' and built around the young person's needs.
- Ensuring that the young people embarking on the programme are motivated and prepared to take part, and do not feel pressured into a mentoring relationship.
- Providing ongoing support and training for mentors, particularly in preparing mentors for the complexity and reality of working with vulnerable pupils.
- Ensuring that parents and families are involved in the programme, and where possible that they have opportunity to get to know their child's mentor.

━━━━━━━━ **THEORY FOCUS 6.2** ━━━━━━━━

### The Zone of Proximal Development (ZPD)

This theory is a concept introduced by psychologist Lev Vygotsky (1896–1934) that describes the gap between what a learner can do independently and what they can do with help.

The zone of proximal development (ZPD) represents the space between what a learner can do unsupported and what the learner cannot do even with support. It's the range where the learner is able to achieve, but only with support from a teacher or a peer with more knowledge or expertise. This person is known as the 'more knowledgeable other'.

Since Vygotsky's original work, the definition for the zone of proximal development has been further developed and modified. It is often acknowledged the teacher helps the student attain the skill the student is trying to master, until the teacher is no longer needed for that task. In the zone of proximal development, we're stretched to learn and grow, without beginning to feel overwhelmed.

Mentoring and coaching provides individuals with scaffolding and guidance. This process enables others to move through their zone of proximal development. Their reflections and insights can lead to personal growth and a deeper understanding of the skill they're trying to attain.

As with all approaches, this model is not without its challenges. For example, it can be challenging to locate the 'sweet spot' of an individual's zone of proximal development. To help someone to move beyond their comfort zone, without stretching them beyond their limitations.

Similarly, this process requires a high level of scaffolding to keep the learner in the zone of proximal development. The mentor or coach needs to have a deep understanding of the individual's wants, needs and skill set. We should also exercise caution here. We want to provide support and scaffold so that the individual is set up for success. The nature of being supported by a 'more knowledge other' may result in the individual becoming over reliant and too dependent on the scaffolding that is provided.

---

## ━━━━━━ CASE STUDY 6.2 ━━━━━━

### Innerscope

*This case study is informed by interviews with James Aidoo, CEO and founder of Innerscope, a London charity that coaches secondary school pupils and supports educators nationwide.*

Innerscope set out to explore how they could influence young people's behaviours through supportive challenge. Guided by the belief that effective change makers draw on multiple sources of influence rather than relying on just one, James Aidoo and his team built their approach on the research of social scientist Joseph Grenny, enabling them to achieve exceptional results and maximise opportunities for pupils. Grenny identified six sources of influence which are based on two basic drivers, motivation and ability. James, was struck by Grenny's holistic approach, which integrates multiple sources of influence to drive behaviour change, he explains:

> By addressing personal, social and structural factors simultaneously, the team now have a comprehensive and effective strategy for achieving sustainable change to behaviour.

Through each source of influence, James and his team seek to answer specific questions in their work with pupils:

1 Personal motivation: Do pupils enjoy what they're being asked to achieve? If not, why not? What are their drivers? How can we leverage this? Can we encourage individuals to engage in the desired behaviour by aligning it with their values and interests?

2 Personal ability: Are they able to achieve their goal? Do they have the necessary skill set to realise their ambition? Can we enhance the young persons' skill set through education and training?

*(Continued)*

3  Social motivation: What are their social drivers? Are pupils negatively influenced by others? Do
   others encourage them to enact poor choices or choices that distract them from their goal. Can
   we leverage social influences through positive peer pressure, role models and social norms to
   encourage the desired behaviour?
4  Social ability: How do we provide pupils with social support and resources, such as coaching,
   mentoring and teamwork, to help young people perform the desired behaviour?
5  Structural motivation: What are the process and systems that will facilitate success? Are rewards
   motivating? What is the role of disincentives to motivate pupils to engage?
6  Structural ability: Is the pupil immersed in an environment that will enable them to reach their
   goal? How do we ensure they're able to access the necessary systems, processes, tool and
   physical spaces?

Innerscope specialises in working with students who are experiencing a range of challenges. This
includes pupils who are not yet realising their full potential, those who are at risk of falling behind
academically, those who struggle to show maturity and take responsibility for their learning and those
who are struggling to gain confidence and build self-esteem.

As an introduction to their comprehensive mentorship programme. Pupils receive a powerful
keynote presentation where James shares the concept of the '4Ps'.

Pupils are invited to reflect and consider whether they recognise any of the following
behaviours:

**Participant:** Someone who is enthusiastic, fully engaged and focussed. These pupils
are positive role models. Pupils who are in the participant zone have managed to
establish and maintain effective relationships with teachers and peers. They can
clearly articulate their drivers for achievement.

**Pioneer:** A pioneer is someone who leads with confidence. These pupils are deeply
intentional and inspiring to others. They're dynamic and empathetic; ready to take on
board another's perspective. These pupils often have a positive ripple effect on their
peers. There's a direct correlation between their positive learning disposition and their
academic outcomes.

**Passenger:** When pupils are in the passenger zone, they've already worked out that if they
quietly stay under the radar, they can avoid being challenged. As a result, they can present
as passive or apathetic. They haven't learnt to take responsibility for their learning yet.
We're at risk of normalising low expectations for these pupils, even though they're capable
of much more. Innerscope offers support through creating a safe space for pupils to
identify their barriers to learning and articulate their reason to achieve. Once these themes
are explored, pupils can demonstrate greater agency of over their learning.

**Protestor:** When pupils are in the protestor zone, it's evident that they're natural leaders
and strong communicators. However, they're yet to harness these attributes effectively and
as result, can find themselves in conflict with teachers and peers. Innerscope has found
that through offering supportive challenge and adopting a strength-based approach,
pupils who are in the protestor zone are able to translate their intention to action.

The '4Ps' are not 'fixed' states, and we move between these roles, according to how we feel at any given point in time. As part of their extensive coaching programme (which includes access to online resources and coaching modules) pupils are given the tools to develop their emotional resilience and intelligence so that they can realise the ambitious goals they set for themselves and unlock their potential.

---

## ══ LINKS TO CLASSROOM PRACTICE 6.2 ══

- How can coaching and mentoring support our young people to achieve their best?
- What processes and mechanisms need to be considered to ensure maximum impact?
- Why is 'person-centred' support integral to the success of designing coaching and mentoring programmes for vulnerable pupils?

---

## ══ CASE STUDY 6.3 ══

## Mentivity

*This case study is informed by interviews with Sayce Holmes-Lewis, founder and CEO of Mentivity, an award-winning mentoring organisation and alternative education provider.*

Founded in 2016 with co-founders Sayce Holmes-Lewis, Leon Wright, and Tyson Holmes-Lewis, Mentivity now works with schools and organisations across the UK, engaging over 400 young people each week. With a focus on empowerment, mentorship and inclusivity, the organisation is dedicated to building community cohesion and nurturing resilient young people, ensuring they have the opportunities and support needed to thrive.

Outreach and services are organised through three main pillars of engagement:

- Mentivity mentoring
- Mentivity House
- Mentivity Respite Provision

The team provides tailored support and offers inclusive spaces where young people can learn, grow and succeed, with a focus on collaboration and holistic development.

## Mentoring

Through personalised 1:1 mentoring and dynamic sessions which take place in small groups, the team create positive learning experiences that empower young people to take responsibility for their choices and ensure their actions are aligned with their goals.

*(Continued)*

Many of the mentees are pupils with special educational needs and a number of children and their families experience multiple vulnerabilities. In some instances, these pupils would traditionally be considered 'at risk' because they have already experienced serious harm or trauma in their lives.

As part of their extensive offer, the team have created several bespoke programmes. This includes their flagship programme, The Raising Aspirations Project (R.A.P), sponsored by Goldman Sachs. The project is designed to guide and steer pupils to discovering career paths that align with their passion and help them achieve their fullest potential.

The Empowerment Programme is focused on sports, well-being and personal development. Aimed at children aged 11–14 years from underserved communities, the programme seeks to develop emotional intelligence, self-awareness and emotional regulation through mindfulness, yoga, sport and mentoring.

As part of Mentivity's collaboration with Croydon's Youth Offending service, the Fundamental Project was launched. The goal is to reduce offending and reoffending, empowering participants to become agents of change and masters of their own destiny. The results are impressive, with only 10% of referrals reoffending, project continues to demonstrate its power and purpose.

## Respite Provision

Mentivity also offers bespoke holistic programmes and alternative provision for pupils who traditionally face limited options within our current educational system (for example managed moves or permanent exclusion). At their respite provision, pupils have the opportunity to re-engage with education, develop essential life and social skills and rediscover a love of learning. A safe space for pupils to develop their resilience with trusted adults, sets children up for success.

The team recognises the urgent need for both professionals and families to be able to access additional resource, acknowledging that some schools face limitations and subsequently struggle to adequately support pupils with complex needs. The team also recognises that vulnerable pupils often face significant delays when attempting to access much needed therapeutic support.

For this reason, Mentivity's approach is trauma informed and underpinned by the six principles of nurture:

- Children's learning is understood developmentally.
- Creating a safe base.
- The importance of nurture for the development of well-being.
- Language is a vital means of communication.
- Understanding behaviour as communication.
- Supporting transition with structure.

Enabling pupils to positively engage with education and develop their academic and social skills.

## Mentivity House

More than a passion, Mentivity House is a personal endeavour for Founder and CEO, Sayce Holmes – Lewis. The 'house' is situated in Aylesbury Estate; the neighbourhood Sayce grew up in and includes state-of-the-art facilities (including a podcast studio sponsored by Spotify). The team are keen to stress this much more than a building or community centre; it is a space to nurture young minds and innovate. Moreover, the team envisage Mentivity House being a catalyst for growth. In addition to hosting a weekly youth club, the space has already become a vibrant hub and a place for community leaders to collaborate.

## Relationships

In keeping with the spirit of community cohesion, Mentivity work closely with two consortia from the My Ends programme in both Southwark and Croydon. An initiative backed by the Mayor's Violence Reduction Unit to enable communities to develop collaborative solutions to counteract the impact of violent crime in their neighbourhoods.

Partnerships with companies such as Avanade (a global professional services company providing IT consulting), ensure that pupils have access to the latest technology and equipment. This partnership provides a pathway for a Microsoft certification in e-learning and access to 'intro to tech' days, offering mentees an insight into the world of business and tech.

As part of their commitment to contributing to the wider sector, Mentivity has also designed a Workforce Upskilling Programme for organisations that are curious about developing their knowledge and skills to mentor effectively.

Mentivity's hyperlocal focus is intentional. As founder and CEO, Sayce – Holmes-Lewis explains, 'Marginalised groups are consistently displaced and pulled apart. It's essential we create a sense of belonging for our young people so they can build a strong sense of self and identity. This work is rooted in empowering communities'.

---

# Summary

This chapter explored the advantages of mentoring, coaching and sponsorship, recognising that these relationships are mutually beneficial. In fact, 87% of both mentors and mentees feel empowered by their mentoring relationships and have developed greater confidence (Wronski, 2019) and mentors themselves are also more than six times more likely to be promoted (Quast, 2012).

We explored mentoring and coaching models and considered systems and structures which have led to profound growth and upskilling. We also acknowledged who was most likely to benefit from these relationships and the moral imperative to provide leaders of Global Majority Heritage (GMH) and other underrepresented groups with pathways into leadership.

These principles can also be applied to pupils. We explored case studies which offered high quality mentoring and coaching experiences for young people, outlining the processes for developing a growth mindset and becoming a resilient learner. We know all pupils, in particular our most vulnerable pupils, benefit.

Whilst the evidence base is still developing, we identified 'what works' and the key ingredients needed for developing lasting, successful mentoring partnerships. Understanding that school-based mentoring is only part of the solution, place-based support demands that we centre our conversations on the needs of young people. Co-designing support that is person-centred and based on the wants and needs of the community we serve.

## Reflective Task

Now that you've completed Chapter 6, take a moment to reflect:

1  Who stands to benefit the most from coaching and mentoring in your setting? How can we make coaching and mentoring accessible for all?
2  What might you need to consider as an individual and as a leadership team to ensure that a high premium is placed on coaching and mentoring?
3  How can coaching and mentoring inform a culture of learning?

# References

Bergmann, J., Alban Conto, C. and Brossard, M. (2022) *Increasing women's representation in school leadership: A promising path towards improving learning.* Florence: UNICEF Office of Research – Innocenti.

Boulton, A. (2024) *Why mentoring is on the rise.* JLL. Available at: https://www.jll.co.uk/en/trends-and-insights/workplace/why-mentoring-is-on-the-rise (Accessed 20 December 2024).

Cantalupo, G. (2022) *Does mentoring still matter for Fortune 500 companies?* Forbes. Available at: https://www.forbes.com/councils/forbescommunicationscouncil/2022/05/19/does-mentoring-still-matter-for-fortune-500-companies/ (Accessed 20 December 2024).

National Institute of Teaching (NIoT) (2023) *Mentoring and coaching of teachers: What can research tell us?* Available at: https://niot.s3.amazonaws.com/documents/NIOT_mentoring_and_coaching_-_Key_Takeaways.pdf (Accessed 20 December 2024).

Quast, L. (2012) *How becoming a mentor can boost your career.* Forbes. Available at: https://www.forbes.com/sites/lisaquast/2011/10/31/how-becoming-a-mentor-can-boost-your-career/#31204bee5f57 (Accessed 20 December 2024).

Sexton, T. (2023) *Why mentoring: What the stats say in 2023.* McCarthy Mentoring. Available at: https://mccarthymentoring.com/why-mentoring-what-the-stats-say-in-2023 (Accessed 20 December 2024).

Shaw, B. and Bernardes, E. (2018) *Forging futures through mentoring: A risk worth pursing?* London: Children's Commissioner.

The Education Endowment Foundation (EEF) (2025) *Mentoring.* Available at: https://educationendowmentfoundation.org.uk/education-evidence/teaching-learning-toolkit/mentoring (Accessed 1 August 2025).

Worth, J., McLean, D. and Sharp, C. (2022) *Racial equality in the teacher workforce: An analysis of representation and progression opportunities from initial teacher training to headship.* NFER. Available at: https://www.nfer.ac.uk/media/hxpdemc4/racial_equality_in_the_teacher_workforce_full_report.pdf (Accessed 1 August 2025).

Wronski, L. (2019) *Nine in 10 workers who have a career mentor say they're happy in their jobs.* CNBC. Available at: https://www.cnbc.com/2019/07/16/nine-in-10-workers-who-have-a-mentor-say-they-are-happy-in-their-jobs.html (Accessed 20 December 2024).

# 7
# Distributed Leadership

---
### Key Terms
---

These terms may be of use in understanding this chapter and subsequently facilitating discussions with colleagues in your school(s).

**Dual-coding** is a strategy for reducing cognitive load that involves linking a visual to a piece of text.

**Interleaving** is a learning strategy that involves mixing different topics or problem types during study sessions instead of focusing on one at a time, enhancing learning and retention by promoting active recall and discrimination between concepts.

**Re-allocated resource:** To strategically redistribute assets, personnel, finances or other resources within the school, so that they align with current demands.

**Outreach** is an effort to bring services or information to people where they spend time or live.

---

## Introduction

Leaders can directly impact the quality of education by shaping the school's culture, but with shrinking budgets and ever-increasing demands on leaders, how do we balance the seemingly impossible task of doing more with less?

The age of the 'hero' headteacher is over. As a sector, we now have a better understanding of the potential pitfalls of 'charismatic' leaders. The omniscient, omnipotent being who has unilateral control of decision-making.

Schools have historically operated under a hierarchical 'top-down' structure. However, research has shown distributed leadership is particularly effective in supporting disadvantaged pupils to make rapid and sustained progress. We know it's also a great mechanism for succession planning.

As the educational landscape continues to evolve, we're seeing increased collaboration across the sector between schools with a variety of governance structures (local authority schools, trusts, federations and independent schools). Consequently, we're also witnessing an increased demand for distributed leadership.

This chapter examines the most recent thinking, theory and research and considers how this can be applied to our own school communities. We also explore case studies from schools in Plymouth and London that have successfully used distributed leadership models to drive school improvement and create a sense of belonging.

# How Can Research Inform Our Practice?

Research can play a vital role in shaping our practice by highlighting how distributed leadership enables leaders to strengthen their teams, make strategic use of resources, foster professional growth, attract and keep strong leaders, and expand their impact beyond the organisation.

## Building Capacity

We're all too familiar with the statistics on teacher workload and well-being. Since this has been included in the inspection framework, there is temptation for leaders to assume more responsibility and lessen the load for others. But this unwittingly reduces teacher autonomy over time and the capacity of the organisation. While it might feel counterintuitive, sharing the load enables teams to achieve their organisational goals without any one individual becoming overloaded. Liu and Werblow (2019) describe the positive effect distributed leadership has on self-efficacy, which consequently improves staff well-being and attitudes to work.

## Re-Allocating Resource

Distributed leadership also presents organisations with an excellent opportunity to consider how they re-allocate resources. Are the most appropriate responsibilities sitting with the correct individual or teams? How is the distribution of responsibility driving efficacy or impacting on morale?

Effective distributed leadership will support shrinking school budgets and enable schools to weather storms such as unexpected resignation and staff illness. Teams are also able to succession plan more effectively when knowledge and expertise is more evenly spread and developed over time.

## Developing Talent and Teams

The inclusive nature of distributed leadership can promote a sense of shared responsibility and empowerment – a particularly powerful tool when we consider the evidence base shows schools are lacking in diversity (Demie et al., 2023). Therefore, utilising distributed leadership to promote equity and signposting aspiring leaders of Global Majority Heritage to opportunities where they can assume responsibility is vital.

Improving pupil outcomes is both necessary and important. However, Galdames-Calderón (2023) explains that teams which promote diversity of thought have the capability to achieve so much more:

> Distributed leadership aligns with the complex and dynamic nature of the modern educational environment. It recognises that no single leader possesses all the knowledge and skills required to address the multifaceted challenges in schools...Instead, distributed leadership taps into the expertise and potential of various individuals, allowing for a more comprehensive and responsive approach to school improvement. (p. 4)

By involving a broader range of perspectives and harnessing a group's collective intelligence, distributed leadership promotes innovative problem-solving, continuous learning, and the ability to adapt to changing educational contexts.

To fully embed distributed leadership, we're required to think carefully and creatively about how to develop our teams.

For example, the appraisal process typically used in schools is necessary and serves an important purpose. But if we're not careful, it can also result in narrow targets that don't help individuals and teams to realise their potential. For this reason, leaders may want to consider how they support staff members to access professional development opportunities that sit outside of the standard appraisal process. Writing personal development plans in collaboration with employees can be a supportive way to achieve this. These plans need to be independent of the appraisal process – a working document that can be considered a 'roadmap' to success. Personalised plans can be a pathway to promotion, a support mechanism to see a project through to completion or realise a goal.

## Recruitment and Retention of Teachers and Leaders

It stands to reason that when teachers feel levels of self-efficacy are high, we can expect to see this reflected in rates of recruitment and retention.

García Torres (2019) explores the relationship between distributed leadership, teacher job satisfaction and pupil outcomes. Schools that increase leadership opportunities for teachers, demonstrate the ability to create positive work environments that enable the most disadvantaged pupils to thrive.

These sentiments are also echoed by Zheng et al. (2019), who explain the importance of narrowing the 'power distance' between members to bring positive managerial change. The result is a collective sense of purpose and agency – a deep connection among the staff and wider school community and a shared understanding that we all have 'skin in the game'.

## Outreach

When practice is strong and distributed leadership is embedded, the team will be ready to share their expertise beyond their own setting.

García Torres (2019) notes distributed leadership offers numerous opportunities for professional collaboration. Increasingly, we are seeing schools carefully curate opportunities for teachers over time so that leaders at all levels can contribute to the wider sector, whether that is through research and curriculum development, school-to-school support or more recent initiatives such as blog posts, articles, national conferences, guest lectures and podcasts.

More established leaders may welcome the opportunity to deliver training, whether that's through informal networks or local teaching school providers offering the Early Career Framework and National Professional Qualifications (NPQs). Teachers and leaders may also want to consider gaining governance experience beyond their own setting, to contribute locally and to further develop their own subject knowledge and expertise. Local authorities are often on the lookout for school leaders to join their SEND and safeguarding boards, again this presents an opportunity to influence the strategic direction of travel in your locality.

Although outreach is an important aspect of professional development for new and established leaders, it can often be overlooked. The protégé effect reminds us that explaining material to others reinforces our own understanding. We can develop leaders through outward-facing opportunities. Through sharing our expertise, we are encouraged to re-examine our own practice and view the provision in our own settings through a new lens. New and established leaders should also be encouraged to develop professional networks beyond their own setting to develop diversity of thought and supportive challenge.

Naturally, there is also a moral imperative to developing outreach. Providing school-to-school support in a changing educational landscape is essential and offers reciprocal benefits.

## ━━━━━━━ CASE STUDY 7.1 ━━━━━━━

## Millbay and High Street Primary School, Plymouth

*This case study is informed by interviews with Steph Macdonald, Executive Headteacher of Millbay and High Street Primary Academies in Plymouth, part of Reach South Academy Trust.*

Under the leadership of Steph Macdonald, High Street Primary School moved from an 'inadequate' Ofsted rating in 2019 to 'good' in all areas by 2023. This rapid and sustained improvement journey took place against the odds. Both High Street and Millbay Primary Academies are described as being in an 'area of deprivation, within an area of deprivation'. With Stonehouse ranked in the top 1% of the most deprived areas in the country, Steph, the leadership team and wider staff body have been delivering education to an underserved and under-resourced community, demonstrating what can be achieved through resilience and collective commitment. Many of her pupils are growing up in homes where they have experienced up to six generations of unemployment and 60% of the immediate locality is made of social housing (compared to 17.5% nationally). 70% of caregivers at High Street have no GCSEs or equivalent and historically there were high levels of mistrust between families and school. However, today's families describe the school as a 'special place' and happily share examples of leaders going 'above and beyond' to help them to support their child's education (Ofsted, 2023).

So how did the team achieve this? Steph is keen to point out that like many school leaders serving communities in areas of high deprivation, she needed to make a little go a long way! Therefore, strategic planning and distributed leadership was essential. The team needed to meet the needs of the community, without breaking the bank.

Steph was appointed Headteacher at High Street Primary in 2021, and her school were subsequently joined by pupils at Millbay (as her setting merged with the primary provision of the local all-through). Managing split sites whilst raising standards, was no easy feat. There was an urgent need to reconsider priorities and establish the vision and culture. It was challenging to know where to start, as everything felt both urgent and important.

Detailed analysis and triangulation revealed that several issues could be traced back to the curriculum. Insufficient challenge contributed to poor outcomes for pupils and on the other end of the spectrum, there were also several pupils who could not access the learning. This was a contributing factor in poor behaviour and the high frequency of behaviour incidents.

In recognition that the curriculum would be a key lever for lifting pupils out of poverty, Steph swiftly set to work establishing new cultural norms and co-constructing teaching and learning principles with the team at High Street.

Building capacity through distributed leadership was an integral part of this plan. Initially core subject leaders were empowered to lead their specialist areas and, in the short term, Steph retained oversight of the non-core subject areas that needed most development. This prevented staff from becoming overwhelmed whilst they returned to 'core teaching principles and fundamentals'.

Steph was clear from the onset that an important part of alleviating teacher workload and building capacity, would be curriculum design. The creation of an accessible, highly structured curriculum that was well resourced and supported adaptive teaching.

Acknowledging that 'what works well for under-resourced pupils and SEND pupils, works well for all pupils', the SENDCO was included in all aspects of curriculum design. Leaders at all levels set about creating a vocabulary rich, contextualised curriculum. A curriculum which met the needs of learners and was reflective of their community.

The structured curriculum, coupled with highly skilled adaptive teaching and sufficient stretch and challenge, meant that over time there was less reliance on interventions. This was important for a small school that needed to do continue doing more, with less.

Pupils now have access to a highly ambitious curriculum. Teachers report that its systematic implementation has reduced teacher workload and supported pupils' knowledge retention over time. This is something that Steph's team are keen to emphasise, rigour does not need to come at the expense of teacher or pupil well-being.

Despite social and economic factors locally, pupils are now thriving at High Street. The team gave considerable thought to how dysregulated learners are prepared for learning. Their answer was to ensure that school became a safe, supportive and highly predictable learning environment. Each day started with a familiar routine and structure, no matter what lesson was being delivered the format was similar. Both pupils and staff knew what to expect. The automaticity of routines reduced cognitive load and supported pupils to learn. Steph explains class teachers were freed up to focus exclusively on the delivery of high-quality teaching.

Re-allocation of resource has been integral to this. For example, class teachers are no longer required to deliver clubs, these are now delivered by external companies, so that pupils' social and cultural capital can be developed.

Teacher's time is also protected throughout the day and working week. They're not required to cover break duties and are offered one full day of PPA per fortnight which can be taken off site. Steph confirms that teachers have the autonomy and agency to complete their work how and when they need to when they're off site, giving them the flexibility to take part in other activities that are traditionally off limits, for example working parents are able to take their children to school.

*(Continued)*

Steph and the team also recognised the importance of utilising distributed leadership to deliver professional development, to sustain the school improvement journey and to grow future leaders.

Professional development meetings (PDMs) were updated to include 'wins and wants', a brief team analysis of what was going well and what the team would like to improve, in relation to the school improvement plan. Each session began with 'strategy snacks' the team's way of efficiently horizon scanning and reviewing current theory and educational research. The main body of the meeting contained clarity of messaging and a clear evidence-based approach to implementation. It was vitally important that no arbitrary updates or messaging made its way into the PDMs. The purpose of the PDM was always to build knowledge, motivate staff, develop teaching techniques or embed practice (See EEF guidance, 2021). In keeping with the school's ethos on equity, teaching assistants also had access to high same high-quality professional development teachers had.

Naturally, school improvement is not without its challenges. Upon assuming her headship Steph recalls engaging with a colleague to rally support only to be told, 'You're the fourth person to have asked me this and, respectfully, all the other headteachers left'.

Winning hearts and minds can be difficult at the best of times. Establishing new cultural norms and distributed leadership is not for the faint hearted. Yet the evidence base shows us that when leaders are prepared to 'practice what they preach' and exhibit their values through their behaviours and small daily interactions, they can build trusting relationships with their teams.

Steph echoes this sentiment. '*From day one, we were clear that we wanted to bring people along with us and we wanted any changes in culture to be fair and equitable*'. This is also reflected in staff attrition rates with high staff turnover (ten teachers in 2022), dropping to only two teaching assistants in 2023. In a testament to school's commitment to recruitment, retention, and professional development pathways, two ECTs have successfully passed their induction and three HLTAs have progressed onto teacher training routes. Providing stability, local employment, raising standards and carving out opportunities for some of the most vulnerable pupils.

---

# ──────── THEORY FOCUS 7.1 ────────

## Social Learning Theory

Social learning theory, or social cognitive theory, was developed by Canadian psychologist Albert Bandura in the 1960s. The theory suggests that learning occurs through observation, imitation and interactions with others. We acquire behaviours, knowledge and skills through our ability to observe others and the consequences of other's actions.

This theory is particularly relevant in the context of distributed leadership, as it reminds us that leadership is not an act that takes place in isolation, rather it's a reciprocal relationship. A series of social exchanges where we can upskill.

Therefore, leadership is not the result of an individual's qualities or personal attributes, instead it is something that develops over time as the result of shared experiences. Whereas traditional models of school leadership may look very hierarchical, more recent models of distributed leadership lend themselves to social learning theory by recognising that expertise and good practice can emerge from any part of an organisation. Leaders who embrace this approach encourage collaboration, knowledge-sharing and diversity of thought, ultimately enhancing teaching practice and pupil outcomes.

When it comes to workplace behaviours, we can capitalise on social learning theory for a range of purposes. For example, we can look to improve professional standards and workplace behaviours through observing and modelling productive behaviours and therefore strengthen the culture.

Naturally, the principles of social learning theory can support pupils' learning too. According to Bandura for learning from observation or modelling to be effective the following conditions need to be in place:

- **Attention**: Learners must focus on the modelled behaviour. Teachers can support this by ensuring materials and learning are accessible, and age appropriate.
- **Retention:** Research into working memory has led to a deepened understanding of how pupils store information. As a result, teachers are now better equipped to facilitate knowledge retention. Strategies such as dual coding, vocabulary exploration, categorisation and interleaving help embed new learning in long-term memory. Teachers will also want to draw upon a range of strategies, for example categorising words and information, making links to prior learning and embedding knowledge through interleaving.
- **Reproduction:** Pupils need numerous opportunities to practice the model and apply any new knowledge. Therefore, it's essential to give pupils plenty of time to rehearse and refine taught knowledge and skills and offer timely feedback.
- **Motivation:** Pupils (like adults), need to be willing to engage with the modelled behaviour or learning and 'give it a go'. Engagement requires appropriate challenge and positive reinforcement. Celebrating effort and resilience encourages persistence.

## ═══ LINKS TO CLASSROOM PRACTICE 7.1 ═══

Leadership teams will want to carefully plan for the implementation of distributed leadership. Whether you're a staff member looking to play a more active role or a school leader looking to introduce more equitable ways of working, here are some questions for consideration:

1 How do we facilitate inclusivity and collaboration?
2 How open are people to sharing ideas and taking on new responsibilities?
3 Are there any power dynamics or hierarchies that might hinder distributed leadership?
4 What is the desired impact we are looking to achieve?
5 What are the potential challenges and opportunities of implementing distributed leadership?
6 What resources and support do we need to successfully implement distributed leadership?

━━━━━━━━ **CASE STUDY 7.2** ━━━━━━━━

## Bowes Primary School, Connect Education Trust, Enfield

*This case study is informed by interviews with Effie Demetriou, Headteacher of Bowes Primary School, part of the Connect Education Trust, Enfield.*

In January 2025, Bowes Primary school was graded outstanding in all areas, with inspectors noting:

> This is a very happy and purposeful school. It wholly succeeds in its ambition to nurture all pupils' hearts and minds. Everyone lives up to the school's core values of resilience, respect and responsibility. Staff and pupils enjoy excellent working relationships. Pupils know that staff will always look out for them, so they feel safe and well cared for.

Yet, Bowes Primary School faces the same challenges so many schools do today, shrinking budgets and increased numbers of SEND pupils joining the provision. All this set against the backdrop of a national recruitment and retention crisis. So how has this been achieved?

Building on the principles of social learning theory, headteacher Effie Demetriou has developed models of distributed leadership which have enabled team members and leaders at all levels to shape policy and practice.

One example of this was the co-creation and development of the school's approach to supporting pupils with behaviour, attitudes and personal development.

The increased numbers of pupils that were presenting with a range of unmet needs had become a challenge. Understandably, teachers and support staff found this difficult. This was also clear from staff well-being surveys in which staff reported increased levels of stress. Like many schools, the initial response was. 'We need more staff!'

Something needed to change. In recognition that the staffing ratio would need to be financially sustainable, Effie took action. She responded by reaching out to the team to better understand what their daily challenges and concerns were. It quickly became apparent that due to the changing needs of each cohort, further training was required. This would empower the team to feel confident they had the skills to support each child, irrespective of the social or emotional starting point.

In keeping with EEF recommendations (2021), the team took part in a carefully planned training over time, including training from renowned behaviour specialist and advisor Paul Dix. In the spirit of collaboration, Effie also invited leaders from Fern House School, a special school within the trust to share their innovate approaches to trauma informed practice.

Then began the more challenging aspect. How to make sense of the learning and translate the theory into practice. Whilst the team felt as though they had benefitted enormously from the professional development, they were yet to determine how they would move forward. For example, colleagues from Fern School had shared some excellent practice and whilst there were some transferrable principles, as a mainstream setting the team didn't have the same resource or facilities. What would a shared approach to 'behaviour' at Bowes look like? How would it be codified?

Effie, collated feedback from the team and set about draughting shared principles, underpinned by the notion that first attention goes to best conduct, with the intention of creating clear, simple routines and expectations. The goal was to ensure children understood they're valued members of the school community and to motivate pupils to always try their best.

It was important that as well as clearly communicating the school values, the guidance provided teachers with descriptors to ensure consistency. As result, there is clarity on how positive behaviours are recognised. For example, positive notes are sent home, children receive mentions in weekly achievement assembly, pupils are acknowledged on class boards and in the spirit of distributed leadership, lunch time staff award marbles which are collected in class jars at lunch time. The class with the most marbles is also celebrated.

Pupils received regular messages home via school postcards, positive phone calls and positive emails and those pupils who go 'above and beyond' have their exceptional behaviour acknowledged with a star badge.

To co-construct the guidance, Effie first had to facilitate a conversation with the team, where they agreed on a shared set of principles or non-negotiables. This included:

- using positive reinforcement with pupils.
- intervening when incidents occur and following restorative approaches where possible.
- all team members following up each time with pupils, retaining ownership and engaging in reflective dialogue with learners.

Number 3 was particularly challenging and required a shift in culture, as in many settings, when staff members felt overwhelmed, tired or frustrated there was a temptation to escalate challenging behaviour to an alternative member of staff or a member of the senior leadership team. This in turn caused those staff members to become overwhelmed and created missed opportunities for pupils to build relationships based on trust and mutual respect with all staff, irrespective of their role or responsibility.

To support staff with this, 'steps to success' were created:

- Step 1 – Reminder: A reminder of the three school values (respect, resilience and responsibility), identifying the one that has been broken. If possible, this conversation takes place privately.
- Step 2 – Warning: A clear verbal caution, where possible this takes place privately.
- Step 3 – Last chance: Speak to the child privately and give them a final chance to engage. Offer a positive choice and refer to previous examples of good behaviour.
- Step 4 – Consequence/repair: An appropriate and proportionate consequence is given during a scripted, short restorative conversation. If the child's behaviour improves after a last chance, a positive outcome is discussed with the child as a result of them taking responsibility.

To support clarity and consistency, scripts are provided which model how to demonstrate assertiveness and still focus on positive behaviours. Crucially, to further support staff to 'retain ownership' of the incident when challenging unwanted behaviours, the team are also provided with scripts on how to deal with difficult behaviours and how to manage restorative conversations.

Initially, the first iteration of the 'steps to success' also included reference to a safe space, a short time for dysregulated children to calm down, either within the classroom or elsewhere, as appropriate. The purpose is for the child to calm down, breathe, look at the situation from a different perspective and compose themselves. However, after trialling the guidance, feedback from the team was stark. Support staff and teachers communicated the need for the 'safe space' option to be

(Continued)

available to pupils during any stage of the 'steps to success'. Effie took this feedback on board, and this aspect was included in the updated guidance.

So, what has been the impact? Well as the inspection team noted, '*Pupils' behaviour, social and character development are superb'*. Effie is keen to point out that this has been a journey and a reflection of the whole school community's commitment to child-centred decision-making. In fact, support staff, teachers and leaders at all levels have been able to influence policy and practice. Effie is keen to emphasise the fidelity to the guidance, because the team have 'skin in the game'. Taking ownership of the process through distributed leadership, meant that it was no longer solely down to the headteacher to articulate 'why' decisions were being made. Rather, the team were invited to refine the processes together. The result? A shared language and shared vocabulary for supporting pupils, underpinned by a shared vision.

---

## ━━━━━ LINKS TO CLASSROOM PRACTICE 7.2 ━━━━━

The cases in this chapter describe how the settings built capacity and re-allocated resources.

- What role did communication play in the planning, implementation and monitoring of the strategies?
- How did leaders successfully co-construct their strategies with their respective teams?
- What challenges did each leadership team have to overcome? How did they achieve this?
- What barriers to distributed leadership might be present in your setting?
- How did each setting benefit from distributed leadership?

---

## Summary

When championed by the headteacher, distributed leadership can play a significant role in developing and maintaining an inclusive school culture. Too often school values and mission statements can feel somewhat removed for employees; however, the teamwork and collaborative decision-making that is involved with distributed leadership can bridge this gap, enabling teams to internalise the common vision for the school.

Incentivising teachers to take on leadership responsibilities creates a sense of school ownership. Not only does this boost productivity, community cohesiveness increases and wellbeing improves. Importantly, it's through distributed leadership that we're able to meet the needs of valued colleagues and our most vulnerable pupils (Liu et al., 2023).

This chapter also explored case studies from across the country, which exemplified the way in which school leaders have used distributed leadership to create a sense of belonging, improve outcomes for pupils and deal with systemic challenges. How will this inform your practice?

---

**Reflective Task**

Now that you've completed Chapter 7, take a moment to reflect.

There are numerous approaches to distributed leadership and finding the right approach for your setting and context is key. Here are some questions you may want to consider within your teams:

1 What distributed leadership approach best suits our school context? What evidence/research will you use to help inform this decision-making?
2 What practical steps can your team take to ensure that all voices are heard and valued?
3 How does your team plan to address potential conflicts or disagreements?
4 What are your distributed leadership goals? What will success look like? How will the team know if they have successfully implemented the distributed leadership model?
5 How will you ensure that everyone on the team understands the overarching goals and their role within the team?

---

# References

Demie, F., Maude, K. and Race, R. (2023) *Ethnic inequality in the teaching workforce in schools: Why it matters*. BERA. Available at: https://www.bera.ac.uk/blog/ethnic-inequality-in-the-teaching-workforce-in-schools-why-it-matters (Accessed 29 August 2025).

Galdames-Calderón, M. (2023) 'Distributed leadership: School principals' practices to promote teachers' professional development for School Improvement', *Education Sciences*, *13*(7), p. 715. https://doi.org/10.3390/educsci13070715

García Torres, D. (2019) 'Distributed leadership, professional collaboration, and teachers' job satisfaction in U.S. schools', *Teaching and Teacher Education*, *79*, pp. 111–123. https://doi.org/10.1016/j.tate.2018.12.001

Liu, J., Qiang, F. and Kang, H. (2023) 'Distributed leadership, self-efficacy and wellbeing in schools: A study of relations among teachers in Shanghai', *Humanities and Social Sciences Communications*, *10*, p. 248. https://doi.org/10.1057/s41599-023-01696-w

Liu, Y. and Werblow, J. (2019) 'The operation of distributed leadership and the relationship with organizational commitment and job satisfaction of principals and teachers', *International Journal of Educational Research*, *96*, pp. 41–55. https://doi.org/10.1016/j.ijer.2019.05.005

Ofsted (2023) *Inspection of High Street Primary Academy*. Available at: https://files.ofsted.gov.uk/v1/file/50228285 (Accessed 29 August 2025).

The Education Endowment Foundation (EEF) (2021) *Effective professional development.* Available at: https://educationendowmentfoundation.org.uk/education-evidence/ guidance-reports/effective-professional-development (Accessed 21 March 2025).

Zheng, X., Yin, H. and Liu, Y. (2019) 'The relationship between distributed leadership and teacher efficacy in China: The mediation of satisfaction and trust', *The Asia-Pacific Education Researcher, 28*(6), pp. 509–518. https://doi.org/10.1007/s40299-019-00451-7

## Further Reading

Bhai, M. and Horoi, I. (2019) 'Teacher characteristics and academic achievement', *Applied Economics, 51*(44), pp. 4781–4799. https://doi.org/10.1080/00036846.2019.1597963

Chetty, R., Friedman, J. N. and Rockoff, J. E. (2014) 'Measuring the impacts of teachers II: Teacher value-added and student outcomes in adulthood', *The American Economic Review, 104*(9), pp. 2633–2679. https://doi.org/10.1257/aer.104.9.2633

Ingersoll, R. M. and May, H. (2012) 'The magnitude, destinations, and determinants of mathematics and science teacher turnover', *Educational Evaluation and Policy Analysis, 34*(4), pp. 435–464. https://doi.org/10.3102/0162373712454326

Nadeem, M. (2024) 'Distributed leadership in educational contexts: A catalyst for school improvement', *Social Sciences & Humanities Open, 9*, p. 100835. https://doi.org/ 10.1016/j.ssaho.2024.100835

# 8

# Flexible Working

## Key Terms

These terms may be of use in understanding this chapter and subsequently facilitating discussions with colleagues in your school(s).

**Work-to-family conflict** occurs when experiences and commitments at work interfere with family life, such as extensive, irregular or inflexible work hours, challenges with workload or other forms of work-related stress.

**Equality:** Each individual or group is given the same allocation or resource or opportunity.

**Equity** recognises that individuals have unique circumstances and therefore require specific allocation of resources and opportunity to achieve a fair outcome.

**Personal Day:** Days of authorised leave during term time which an employer chooses to award to employees in school.

**Lieu time/time in lieu:** Paid time off work for having worked additional hours.

## Introduction

Visionary leader and CEO Ricardo Semler believes that for employees to be motivated at work, they must feel a sense of purpose.

He maintains it's the employer's responsibility to promote accountability and trust in the workplace, recognising a nuanced approach to workforce design, results in higher levels of engagement (Semler, 2014). An area that's particularly tricky for school leaders to navigate.

Challenges concerning the teacher labour market are widely documented and we continue to experience a national recruitment and retention crisis.

More recently school leaders are receiving increasing numbers of flexible working requests and we're experiencing a change in attitudes towards remote working, hybrid working and alternative work patterns.

So why has the sector been so slow to respond?

Despite a growing willingness to explore alternative working patterns, without a blueprint or roadmap outlining how this can be achieved, it can feel like a daunting, if not impossible task for school leaders.

Yet the evidence base suggests the benefits for all stakeholders are significant.

In this chapter, we'll explore current research and theory and examine case studies from across the sector. This chapter also offers practical advice and support for leaders on how to successfully implement flexible working.

## How Can Research Inform Our Practice?

Unfortunately, we're all too familiar with the statistics around teacher recruitment and retention. In its annual report into the state of the teacher labour market, the National Foundation for Educational Research (McLean et al., 2024) found that:

- 44% more teachers stated they intended to leave teaching in 2022/2023 than the previous year.
- In 2023/2024 the secondary sector reached half of its target.
- In 2024/2025, 10 out of 17 secondary subjects were forecast to under-recruit.

The report acknowledges the challenges related to teacher pay and workload and recognises remote and hybrid working remains more prevalent in the wider graduate labour market than in teaching. This raises questions for school leaders about the need to re-imagine flexible working opportunities to ensure we have a sustainable workforce (McLean et al., 2024).

## Why Flexible Working for Schools?

An increasing number of employees would like to benefit from working flexibly. A lack of flexibility can prompt some employees to look for a new job or even leave the profession altogether. Alternative work patterns can support employers to:

- address skills shortages.
- attract and retain talent and support diversity.
- narrow the gender pay gap.
- improve employee job satisfaction and motivation.
- support employee well-being and work–life balance.

Robust systems and policies empower organisations to become more agile and responsive to changing demographics and expectations.

### Understanding Work Patterns

Flexible working arrangements can typically be organised into the following categories:

- Hybrid working – The employee completes work on-site or off-site. How the work is completed can take precedence over location. An increasingly common approach for teachers, leaders and those in pastoral or administrative roles in school settings.
- Telecommuting/Remote working – The terms are often used interchangeably however Telecommuters often live close enough to attend meetings in person,

while remote workers are not typically expected to attend meetings in person, though they may attend virtually. Remote working will often refer to working from home but may include working in public or co-working spaces.

- Compressed/condensed hours – the employee completes their standard contracted hours over fewer days. For example, compressing a five-day week into a four-day week, where each individual day is longer, though specific arrangements will vary.
- Flexitime (or staggered hours) – the employee has a degree of flexibility about when their working day starts and finishes, provided they complete their contractual hours. For example, an eight-hour working day may be between 7 a.m. and 3 p.m. or 10 a.m. and 6 p.m., supporting other commitments such as caring responsibilities or additional study.
- Part-time work – Any form of employment that provides fewer weekly hours than a full-time job, typically less than 30 hours per week.
- Shift work – An arrangement where the working hours are divided into shifts, enabling coverage at different times. A popular choice when allocating work streams for premises staff and IT teams to ensure the operational continuity.
- Job sharing – An alternative work pattern which typically involves two people employed on a part-time basis, collaborating to share the responsibilities of one full-time role.
- Term-time only contracts – employees are only expected to attend work during term time. Often a popular choice for working parents.
- Annualised hours – Working hours spread across the year, which may include some school closure days, or where hours vary across the year to suit the school and employee.

## What Are the Benefits for Employers and Employees?

Although school leaders may support flexible working in principle, in practice the sector has been slow to realise the potential of alternative working patterns. However, research shows that flexible working can contribute to reduced workplace stress, improved employee engagement and job satisfaction, as well as reduce sickness absence and lessen work-family conflict (Halpern, 2005).

Employees who are afforded flexibility report higher life satisfaction, better recovery from work and reduced strain. Women in particular benefit; high stress combined with control over working hours results in lower absence rates than high stress with less control (Ala-Mursula et al., 2005).

Implementing flexible working can also result in cost efficiencies. Schools can reap financial benefits through reduced turnover and improved morale (Possenriede and Plantenga, 2014).

Contrary to popular belief, stress and work-family conflict is less to do with long working hours and more to do with the degree of control over your working pattern (Hughes and Parkes, 2007). This is particularly welcome news for senior leaders and executives who recognise the complex nature of their roles and want to protect their well-being by exercising some autonomy over how and when their work is completed.

When staff members are empowered to work at times most favourable to them, and to take breaks when needed it reduces potential accumulation of strain and enables them to maintain well-being.

Schools may need to review their existing practice to accommodate flexible working requests. Leaders will want to take a range of factors into account including: cost, team workload and alternative staffing arrangements – such as overtime to ensure sustainability. Once this exercise has taken place, all stakeholders can be assured the offer is financially sustainable and feasible for both employer and employee.

## Promoting Equity, Diversity, and Inclusion

It's important to note that strong Equality, Diversity and Inclusion (EDI) strategies include equitable approaches to flexible working. Equitable organisations understand this as an integral part of their practice.

We know that flexible working significantly enhances an employer's ability to demonstrate inclusive practice. A comprehensive offer enables employees to apply for roles that they may not otherwise have been able to apply for, including those managing a long-term health illness or disability, carers, working parents or those choosing to pursue alternative goals, such as additional study.

The insurance firm, Zurich, conducted a trial advertising roles with flexible options and gender-neutral language. It increased women's applications for roles by 16% and senior roles by 19%, it's worth noting however, that the company received more than double the typical volume of applications from both men and women when the changes were introduced. The study also noted that part-time employees' sense of belonging increased by 8%, indicating that offering flexible working fosters inclusion and belonging generally (Hacohen et al., 2020).

Similarly, Wharton School (University of Pennsylvania) research found STEM roles offering remote work increased applicants from Global Majority Heritage by 33% and female applicants by 15% (Hsu and Tambe, 2025). While this research was focused on tech start-ups, these findings highlight transferable lessons for the education sector, suggesting thoughtful flexible working policies can enhance diversity, equity and inclusion.

## Barriers to Flexible Working

As a result of recent changes to the Teacher's Pension Service (TPS) it's now easier for employees to request phased retirement. The TPS changes offer older teachers the opportunity to reduce their hours and/or their responsibilities as they approach retirement, but this is only possible if schools wish to employ them.

Data from the headteachers as employers survey shows that headteachers' attitudes to this varied significantly. Nearly a quarter of teachers interviewed were considering remaining longer in teaching and reducing their hours and many expressed a preference for simply being able to reduce their hours. Even though their headteachers expressed support in principle, in practice employees encountered numerous barriers and requests were often denied for a range of reasons, for example lack of continuity for pupils or challenges with timetabling (Peters et al., 2008).

As the teaching profession continues to battle with recruitment and retention, it seems timely to explore alternative working patterns that enable to the sector to retain highly skilled, experienced professionals who still have much to offer the profession.

## ━━━━━━━━ CASE STUDY 8.1 ━━━━━━━━

### Charles Dickens Primary School, Charter Schools Educational Trust

*This case study is informed by interviews with Michael Eggleton, Executive Headteacher of Charles Dickens Primary School, Southwark, a lead school in the London Region for flexible working accreditation.*

Charles Dickens Primary School, part of the Charter Schools Educational Trust, has been awarded its second Department for Education accreditation as a Flexible Working Ambassador School. Accredited schools must demonstrate systems that provide equitable, structured flexible working opportunities rather than ad hoc arrangements. Since 2022, the school has supported other schools and Trusts in reviewing and improving their flexible working practices, demonstrating systems that provide equitable, sustainable opportunities.

### Myth Busting

Headteacher Michael Eggleton stresses that 'this is not a case of one size fits all'. He recognises the challenges that school leaders can face in implementing flexible working and is keen to emphasise how strategies can be adapted according to each context. More recently larger schools, in particular secondary schools are also turning to artificial technology (AI) to support with timetabling. This has proven helpful for leaders who need to balance the complexities of scheduling lessons and flexible working requests, without compromising on provision for pupils.

He also acknowledges this need not be 'feast or famine'. Leaders can explore degrees of flexibility such as hybrid professional development and granting ad hoc requests for special leave which enable staff members to attend personal appointments. Michael explains:

If teachers joining the profession feel as though they're not able to have a life beyond work, protect their well-being and manage competing priorities, then we won't be able to tackle the recruitment and retention challenges that lie ahead.

### How Does This Work in Practice?

The leadership team at Charles Dickens Primary believe that the solution lies in systemic change. As a result, the policy and processes to facilitate flexible working are clear and transparent. The school has a 'solutions focused approach' and all flexible working requests will be considered. Applicants understand that any flexible working arrangement needs to work for both parties (employer and

*(Continued)*

employee). All flexible working requests are agreed for a fixed term and reviewed regularly. This also provides an opportunity for both parties to discuss what is working well and what, if any, adaptations need to be made. Codifying these systems and processes has ensured there is equitable approach.

## What Impact Has This Had?

Leaders have seen the positive impact this has had on staff retention. This is reflected in the enthusiastic way team members describe flexible working, such as Dr. Amy Mulvenna, Head of Art at Charles Dickens Primary School:

> Flexible working has allowed me to work part time whilst completing my PHD. I have now returned to full time teaching and see the benefits of my continued professional development and how this continues to enrich my practice. (Mulvenna, n.d.)

In addition to flexible working arrangements, staff are offered 'stay interviews', an interesting inversion on the traditional exit interview. The meetings are independent of the appraisal process and enable senior leaders to understand employee's aspirations or goals for the future. The interviews have also had positive impact on retention and enabled the school to keep highly skilled teachers in the profession.

Staff are also gifted a 'personal day', this is half a day each term to spend as they please with 'no questions asked'. The leadership team recognised that they were able to cover staff sickness absence at short notice and therefore had the capacity to cover short spells of infrequent absence that had been planned.

# How Can I Successfully Implement Flexible Working?

Successful implementation of flexible working is dependent upon robust systems and policies, underpinned by a strong culture and working practices. This will result in processes which are equitable, transparent and benefit both employer and employee.

## Top Tips for Designing Your School or Trust's Flexible Working Policy

1 Assess needs and preferences: It's essential to understand the needs of your workforce and the needs of your organisation when designing your policy. Are you aware of what working patterns are in demand in your setting and why? Can you reasonably accommodate these and what would the impact be on the day-to-day operational running of the school, academy or Trust? You may find it useful to carry out a survey, interview or hold focus groups to gather intel and understand the needs of your staff body.

2 Consider the legal implications: Ensure that you are fully aware of any legal and regulatory requirements and consult with your Human Resources provider to ensure your policy is compliant and to avoid and legal challenges later. From 6 April 2024, any employee has the right to make a statutory flexible working request from the first day of their employment (although this does not cover the recruitment period) and an employee can make two requests under the statutory regime in any 12-month period. Employees can request a change to:

   i  the number of hours they work.

  ii  when they start or finish work.

 iii  the days they work.

 iv  where they work.

This is known as making a statutory application.

3 Define eligibility: Each application for flexible working must be considered own its on merit. However, to ensure smooth operational and strategic function, you may want to determine the criteria for eligibility based on roles, responsibilities and the needs of your setting. For example, are there specific roles that make flexible working less feasible or core hours that staff are required to be on-site? By clearly defining who is eligible and setting clear expectations, employers can offer a range of working patterns without comprising standards.

4 Determine your flexible working offer: Now it's time to decide to on what your organisation's flexible working offer will be. What working patterns can you reasonably make available to staff? Remember to assess the feasibility of each option according to your setting's needs, the requirements of the various roles in your organisation and take into consideration feedback from stakeholders, so that the policy reflects employee's preferences.

5 Establish core hours: Is it in the best interests of the organisation for all staff to be on-site during set hours or for a set period? These are your core hours. You may decide that staff members are not required to be on-site during core hours but must be available for communication. Setting out clear guidelines for staff and avoiding ambiguity will enable you to strike a healthy balance between flexibility and high-quality collaboration and productivity.

Once you're satisfied you have clear processes and systems in place, it is important to clarify expectations when offering flexible working. Naturally, all employees are subject to the same accountability systems, framework and processes that exist in your setting. Set expectations around maintaining high levels of productivity and take time to consider how you will track outcomes.

## Strategies for Successful Hybrid Working

In their 2021 report, *Flexible working: Lessons from the pandemic*, the CIPD (the professional body for human resources and people development) identified seven strategies for staff and leaders to use to ensure hybrid working is successful:

- Develop the skills and culture needed for open conversations about well-being.
- Encourage boundary-setting and routines to improve well-being and prevent overwork.
- Ensure effective co-ordination of tasks and task-related communication.
- Pay special attention to creativity, brainstorming and problem-solving tasks.
- Build in time, including face-to-face time, for team cohesion and organisational belonging.
- Facilitate networking and inter-team relationships.
- Organise a wider support network to compensate for the loss of informal learning (CIPD, 2021).

Notably, the CIPD stress the importance of appropriate allocation of tasks to those who have been offered flexitime and those who are working remotely. The pandemic shone a light on the distinction between flexibility of hours and flexibility of location. Some tasks can be performed anywhere, whilst other tasks require the employee to be on-site (for example opening and closing the premises). Similarly, some tasks can be performed at any time, whilst other tasks, may need to be completed at specific times (for example checking the register or first day absence calls).

## ━━━━━━ CASE STUDY 8.2 ━━━━━━

### Dixons Academy Trust

*This case study is informed by interviews with Luke Sparkes, Trust Leader at Dixons Academies Trust, driving culture, agility, and innovative workforce design across schools in Leeds, Bradford, Manchester, and Liverpool.*

To many, Dixons Academies Trust are seen as 'positive disruptors' within the sector. The Trust already has a flexible working offer; however, Luke Sparkes is keen to develop this further. He explains:

> The future of education belongs to organisations that are agile enough to evolve and intentional about getting culture right from the start.

There is much discussion about a recruitment and retention crisis, but what if the crux of the issue is much deeper than this? As a sector can we begin to think more creatively about work force design? This cultural shift is powerfully articulated through the trust's trifecta, which has three central tracks:

- Prepare – organisational health.
- Plan – organisational design.
- Proceed – organisational agility.

The trust recognises organisational agility is contingent on a strong culture and has taken intentional steps to move away from traditional approaches to leading, deviating from the 'top down', command and control model. Instead choosing 'sense and respond', an approach that reduces bureaucracy and ensures the right people are working on the right thing, in the right way. Recognising leaders are there to provide insight, understanding and support, rather than 'controlling' their teams. This has enabled the trust to make bold moves and give teaching teams agency.

As a result, from September 2024, the Trust began to move to a 9-day fortnight for teaching staff. The leadership team looked beyond the education sector to learn from other professions that already had established creative flexible working models in place. Luke notes: 'This proposal has generated great excitement in the area and re-invigorated the team after a challenging period post pandemic. We are confident this will lead to further innovation'.

The leadership team have created a culture of aligned autonomy, rather than a homogenised approach. In keeping with this spirit, each of the 17 headteachers within the Trust has rolled out the initiative in the way that is most appropriate for their setting and context. Some of the schools participating are situated in areas which have traditionally found it particularly hard to recruit. These schools have already reported an increase in applications for vacant posts.

## What Does the Future Hold?

The leadership team at Dixons expect working patterns to look very different. Experts in the field anticipate traditional teaching methods and practices to be defined by two key features:

- Teaching teams: Dedicated teams of trained teachers or adults delivering lessons to groups of pupils rather than over reliance on one adult. This may alleviate pressure on succession planning and support pupil well-being, increasing the odds of a child making a connection with a trusted adult.
- Technology: The most obvious way to introduce flexibility to staff working patterns is to hire more teachers. However, school budgets are already stretched, and it is unlikely that this will change in the near future. As technology advances, so may the demand for 'supervised remote learning' particularly at secondary. Interestingly, this may coincide with further developments in artificial intelligence (AI).

We're experiencing a change in attitudes, and there's now widespread perception among teachers and school leaders that increasing the availability of flexible working could improve teacher retention, however there is currently an absence of evidence. It's encouraging that thought leaders such as Dixon's are leading the way, collaborating with the Educational Endowment Fund to take part in a fully funded 'School Choices' project, the sector eagerly awaits the outcome of these findings.

---

## ━━━━━ THEORY FOCUS 8.1 ━━━━━

### Conservation of Resource Theory (COR)

COR theory, devised by Steven Hobfoll in the 1980s (Hobfoll, 1989), describes our relationship to stress. It suggests that psychological stress occurs as a result of three possible scenarios:

1  the threat of a loss of resource.
2  actual loss of resource.
3  a lack of resource having expended significant effort or resource.

*(Continued)*

In this instance, resource can be defined as anything that the employee values or holds dear, a specific object or a state or condition. Hobfall states that the loss of these resources will initiate a stress response.

A balance between professional responsibilities and personal life can be viewed as a highly valued resource. When employees are depleted, this can lead to burnout and reduced performance. COR theory suggests that employees experience conflict when the demands of work drain the resources needed to meet the demands of home life, or vice versa. Work life and home life compete for time, energy and attention. Therefore, alternative working patterns are considered a useful tool for employers and can lead to a reduction in anxiety for employees.

---

## ■ CASE STUDY 8.3 ■

## St. Paul's Way Trust School, University Schools Trust, East London

*This case study is informed by interviews with Firdusi Uddin, Head of School (Secondary & Sixth Form) at St. Paul's Way Trust School, part of the University Schools Trust.*

St. Paul's Way School is a large all-through school in Tower Hamlets, East London. The school is committed to championing diversity, equality and inclusion and leaders model 'future-focussed thinking'.

Across the secondary phase, teachers are entitled to 17% Planning Preparation Assessment (PPA), significantly higher than the national average. Teachers and support staff can work flexibly in several ways, for example from September teachers and leaders with additional responsibility are offered 100 minutes of PPA from home every fortnight. There are also informal arrangements in place for staff members to work from home when completing time sensitive work that requires uninterrupted focus. Sabbaticals, career breaks and secondments are also encouraged.

These initiatives are borne out of the school values:

- Aspiration: We aim for our individual and collective best work with passion and commitment to achieve this.
- Integrity: We do the right thing; even when it's hard; even when no one is watching.
- Community: We make our school a safe and purposeful place where everyone belongs, contributes and thrives.

The leadership team quickly recognised the conditions and culture of the school needed to be conducive to flexible working arrangements before any changes were introduced. School and Trust leaders are keen to iterate; the school has been on a journey. It was imperative that any change was 'done with' and 'not to' the staff body. This was a collaborative effort and as a result there is now collective buy in at the school and recognition that processes have been co-produced, resulting in parity for the team.

Over time this has had a positive impact on staff well-being, staff retention and recruitment. It' has also resulted in cost efficiencies over time, as staff who have had significant time, energy and resource invested in them are less likely to leave and be replaced with inexperienced staff.

Flexible working has also protected the school and Trust from a talent drain, as expert teachers and leaders report feeling valued. They know they're trusted to work autonomously where appropriate, whilst still executing their work to extraordinarily high standard.

Careers Education and Guidance Manager, Kawtar El Ouaraini explains:

> My flexible working arrangements have helped me to balance my workload effectively. My role can be fast paced as I complete student facing and administrative tasks as well as planning and coordinating events. Working flexibly has allowed me to prioritise my workload and maximise my productivity so that I am able to complete my administrative tasks and participate in external meetings. My line manager and the Trust have been supportive of my flexible working requests. This has given my morale a boost as I feel trusted to complete my duties to a high standard.

---

============ **LINKS TO CLASSROOM PRACTICE 8.1** ============

- What commonalities can you identify in all three case studies?
- How did the culture and climate in each setting facilitate flexible working?
- What steps did school leaders take to understand the needs, wants and future of goals of their team?
- What steps did school leaders take to overcome the perceived barriers to flexible working?
- What impact did leaders report this has had?
- What impact did employees report this has had?

---

# Summary

In this chapter, we considered the relationship between flexible work patterns and improved well-being, exploring how research and theory has influenced practice over time.

Clear processes, systems and policies can support the successful implementation of flexible working, but unless these are underpinned by a strong culture which fosters psychological safety and prioritises well-being, they're unlikely to have meaningful impact.

In schools and settings where this practice is well established, the benefits of alternative working patterns for both employees and the employer have been communicated to all stakeholders.

For schools this is an opportunity to demonstrate you're an equitable employer who understands that when employees have a degree of autonomy and agency in their professional lives, they feel better and experience less work–family conflict.

Of course, the benefits are not limited to employees. This chapter explored the significant benefits for employers too, including reduced staff absence and higher levels of engagement.

Through case studies we examined different approaches to flexible working. Leaders explained the importance of finding creative ways to say 'yes' (wherever possible) to alternative working patterns and utilising professional networks for support. Settings with a proven track record of implementation describe the importance of sharing success stories among support staff, teachers and leaders alike and the positive impact this has had on recruitment and retention.

It's easy to find reasons not to engage with flexible working. Schools describe tackling timetables; scaling offers according to the school context or size and the difficulty of ensuring any offer is financially sustainable. However, the benefits outweigh the challenges.

If we want to be seen as a competitive employer of choice, the sector will need to adopt flexible working practices with greater efficiency and commitment.

Then there's also the moral imperative. How equitable is our practice?

Research shows that equality, equity and diversity is better for everyone (Hunt, 2015). We all benefit from a diverse workforce, so how can our flexible working policies facilitate this? Whose voice is missing? After all, a high performing team requires diversity of thought.

## Reflective Task

Now that you've completed Chapter 8, take a moment to reflect:

1 What types of flexible work arrangements are currently being provided in your workplace and how are they communicated to staff?
2 Are there any key barriers to enhancing flexibility in work arrangements? For employees? For employers? If so, how can they be addressed?
3 What kinds of flexible work arrangements would help employees better balance work, family and other personal responsibilities?
4 From an employer standpoint, what benefits do flexible work arrangements provide? Have any unintended consequences resulted from providing employees with greater flexibility?
5 How can flexible work arrangements help employees and employers to engage in equitable practices?

# References

Ala-Mursula, L., Vahtera, J., Linna, A., Pentti, J. and Kivimäki, M. (2005) 'Employee worktime control moderates the effects of job strain and effort-reward imbalance on sickness absence: The 10-town study', *Journal of Epidemiology and Community Health, 59*(10), pp. 851–857. https://doi.org/10.1136/jech.2004.030924

CIPD (2021) *Flexible working – lessons from the pandemic.* Available at: https://www.cipd.org/uk/knowledge/reports/flexible-working-lessons-pandemic/ (Accessed 21 October 2024).

Hacohen, R., Davidson, S., Roy-Chowdhury, V., Bogiatzis-Gibbons, D., Burd, H. and Likki, T. (2020) *Changing the default: A field trial with Zurich insurance to advertise all jobs as part-time.* Available at: https://www.gov.uk/government/publications/a-field-trial-with-zurich-insurance-to-advertise-all-jobs-as-part-time/ (Accessed 21 October 2024).

Halpern, D. F. (2005) 'How time-flexible work policies can reduce stress, improve health, and save money', *Stress and Health, 21*, pp. 157–168. https://doi.org/10.1002/smi.1049

Hobfoll, S. E. (1989) 'Conservation of resources: A new attempt at conceptualizing stress', *American Psychologist, 44*(3), p. 513.

Hsu, D. H. and Tambe, P. B. (2025) 'Remote work and job applicant diversity: Evidence from technology startups', *Management Science, 71*(1), pp. 595–614.

Hughes, E. L. and Parkes, K. R. (2007) 'Work hours and well-being: The roles of work-time control and work-family interference', *Work & Stress, 21*(3), pp. 264–278. https://doi.org/10.1080/02678370701667242

Hunt, D. V., Layton, D. and Prince, S. (2015) *Why diversity matters.* McKinsey & Company. Available at: https://www.mckinsey.com/capabilities/people-and-organizational-performance/our-insights/why-diversity-matters (Accessed 21 October 2024).

McLean, D., Worth, J. and Smith, A. (2024) *Teacher labour market in England annual report 2024.* NFER. Available at: https://www.nfer.ac.uk/publications/teacher-labour-market-in-england-annual-report-2024/?web=1 (Accessed 21 October 2024).

Mulvenna, A. (n.d.) *Flexible working, London south teaching school hub.* Available at: https://www.londonsouthtsh.org/flexible-working (Accessed 21 October 2024).

Peters, M., Hutchings, M., Edwards, G., Minty, S., Seeds, K. and Smart, S. (2008) *Behavioural impact of changes in the teachers' pension scheme* (Research Report No. DCSF-RR024). Available at: https://dera.ioe.ac.uk/id/eprint/7913/ (Accessed 21 October 2024).

Possenriede, D. S. and Plantenga, J. (2014) *Temporal and locational flexibility of work, working-time fit, and job satisfaction* (IZA Discussion Paper No. 8436). Available at: https://www.iza.org/publications/dp/8436/temporal-and-locational-flexibility-of-work-working-time-fit-and-job-satisfaction (Accessed 21 October 2024).

Semler, R. (2014) *How to run a company with (almost) no rules.* TED. Available at: https://www.ted.com/talks/ricardo_semler_how_to_run_a_company_with_almost_no_rules?subtitle=en (Accessed 21 October 2024).

## Further Reading

Dubois, H. and Anderson, R. (2014) *Foundation findings: Work preferences after 50.*
    Eurofound. Available at: https://www.eurofound.europa.eu/en/publications/2014/
    foundation-findings-work-preferences-after-50 (Accessed 21 October 2024).
Wilkens, M., Cabrita, J., Jungblut, J.-M. and Anderson, R. (2018) *Striking a balance:*
    *Reconciling work and life in the EU.* Eurofound. Available at: https://
    www.eurofound.europa.eu/en/publications/2018/striking-balance-reconciling-
    work-and-life-eu (Accessed 21 October 2024).

# 9

# Innovate

---

## Key Terms

These terms may be of use in understanding this chapter and subsequently facilitating discussions with colleagues in your school(s).

**A smart mob** is a group whose coordination and communication abilities have been empowered by digital communication technologies.

**An affinity group** is a group formed around a shared interest or common goal, to which individuals formally or informally belong.

**Environmental scanning** is a strategic process where organisations systematically gather and analyse information about how to identify potential opportunities and threats in the near term. These may come from within the organisation or they may be external.

**Horizon scanning** is the strategic process of identifying emerging threats and opportunities within the sector. These are issues that may arise in the future or long term.

---

## Introduction

Innovation is integral to society. As educators, we're ambitious for the young people we teach and the communities we serve. In addition to meeting key performance indicators and targets set by regulatory bodies such as Ofsted, we're required to prepare pupils for 'life beyond the school gates'. That includes preparing children for employment opportunities that are still being developed and a world that is rapidly changing, thanks to emerging technologies and globalisation.

So how should leaders prepare pupils for the challenges that lie ahead? There's lively debate about what exactly constitutes 'essential learning' and the need for further revisions in response to the recent *Curriculum and Assessment Review* (DfE, 2025). There is consensus though, that moving forwards, pupils will need a rich knowledge base and transferable life skills, such as the ability to critically evaluate and demonstrate resilience. Both of which require a growth mindset.

In this chapter, we examine the way in which innovation can empower individuals and communities, enabling them to face unprecedented challenges. We explore research and theories that promote new ways of working and learn from leading experts across the sector driving innovation.

## How Can Research Inform Our Practice?

We've already looked at the 'bigger picture' and determined that innovation is beneficial for pupils as they move through their school career and of course, for society. But what are the more immediate benefits for learners and educators? How do we define innovation and with increasing demands on our time, should we really be prioritising this?

Innovation plays a very distinct role in education compared to the private sector. Schools often focus on improving learning outcomes and the educational experience, while in the private sector, it's primarily driven by profit and market needs.

Over time, the sector has seen a range of approaches to pedagogy emerge. Organisational structures and processes which drive efficiency have also been developed. These are designed to increase productivity, raise standards and improve the life chances for pupils, particularly pupils from disadvantaged backgrounds and those with special educational needs.

Innovative practice has continued to develop over time. This is evident when we compare the education sector to other industries but it's also true when we consider educational practices in their own right. In 2014, the OECD's report on measuring innovation found:

- 70% of graduates employed in the education sector consider their establishments as highly innovative.
- When it comes to adopting new practices and speed of innovation, higher education stands out with 46% of education professionals reporting that their setting was largely at the forefront of adopting innovative solutions (compared to 31% in primary education and 30% in secondary education).
- Increased collaboration across the sector has become a driving force in developing innovative practice. This has been influenced by peer discussions about instruction and coaching, and more regular opportunities to observe practice (Vincent-Lancrin et al., 2014).

More recently between 2001 and 2011 there was an increase in the range of pedagogical practices internationally which promoted pupils' higher order thinking skills, reasoning and problem-solving skills and the adaptation and personalisation of teaching. This is true across subjects and year groups. Over the subsequent decade innovation at system level and classroom level was more moderate.

Research shows that countries which changed their pedagogical practices the most, typically showed improvements in academic outcomes (the outlier here was maths in secondary provision) (Vincent-Lancrin et al., 2019).

On average, countries that invested in innovate practice reported increased pupil satisfaction and enjoyment at school. Typically, teachers positively associated innovation with self-efficacy. However, there was no consistent correlation between innovation and the reduction of educational inequality. That's not to say it cannot be a mechanism for equity, simply that outcomes were variable in this specific data set (Vincent-Lancrin et al., 2019).

# What Are the Catalysts for Innovation?

The OECD's 2019 report on measuring innovation in education (Vincent-Lancrin et al., 2019), recognises there are numerous drivers for innovation. It can be spurred on by system level change such as the introduction of new legislation, policy reform or new initiatives from Ofsted. Of course, these changes are mandated and must be adopted.

Peer learning and collective learning are also powerful drivers of innovation and they're on the increase, as the sector continues to shift towards a more evidenced-informed approach.

Finally, an identified need at classroom or local level can be the catalyst for innovation; the pathway to finding solutions to some of our most persistent challenges in education.

These can be broken down further as we examine the key proponents for innovation.

## Human Resources

Ultimately innovation requires innovative thinkers who can carry out this important work and champion change, teachers and leaders who have open hearts and minds and the professional curiosity to learn from others. These practitioners also need capacity and carefully thought through policies, to enable them to manage the complex processes involved with change management.

## Learning Organisations

There's a correlation between organisations that have a strong professional climates and innovation. These organisations have robust cultures that are conducive to learning. Leaders will want to give careful consideration as to how work and professional learning is organised so that teachers' development is not hindered by cognitive overload.

## Technology

Over time, we've seen how the introduction of technology has shaped and informed practice for teachers and pupils, driving efficiencies and when used effectively, contributing to improved outcomes. The increase of ambitious digital learning strategies is indicative of the innovative practice that is developing nationally.

## System Organisation

Creating the right conditions for innovation is one thing, but in order for professionals and pupils to reap the benefits over time, school leaders will want to have a clear vision and process for implementing innovative practice. Often, the need to de-implement practices which are no longer useful is overlooked. De-implementation prevents staff from becoming overwhelmed with unnecessary practices that are no are no longer having a positive impact.

## Educational Research

We're seeing increasing numbers of teachers turn to research. This shift in thinking has been accelerated by the increasing 'professionalisation' of the sector. For example, the introduction of the Early Careers Framework (ECF) and the National Professional Qualifications (NPQs) both of which are rooted in evidence, and the emergence of organisations such as the Charted College of Teaching, the professional body for teachers.

## Education Development

An identified need at classroom or local level can also result in innovative changes to practice. Typically, these are persistent challenges that require creative thinking or an unorthodox approach. The sector continues to produce educational organisations that place a high premium on investing and fostering innovation and new approaches to pedagogy.

# What Are the Barriers to Innovation?

It isn't uncommon for policymakers to suggest that schools are slow to adopt certain reforms and make sufficient adaptations. Speak to most experienced leaders though, and they'll quickly confirm that they've seen many superficial policy changes over the years. Some leaders express concern that there have been too many policy changes which haven't been fully thought through and reforms which haven't been rooted in evidence or involved sufficient stakeholder engagement. In this instance, school leaders report frustration and concern that there isn't enough time to embed practice before being held to account or asked to demonstrate impact. Hence the importance of measuring 'what works'.

Of course there are challenges at local level too. For example, a school's capacity or appetite for change and innovation can be influenced by social context, strain on resources, stakeholder engagement, community support, skill set and staff mobility.

## The Role of Psychological Safety

We need psychological safety for innovation to thrive. However, the leader's role in facilitating innovation is often misunderstood. If we're specifically looking to create the right conditions and create a professional climate that is conducive for innovation, we would serve our school communities well, by playing close attention to these six drivers.

### Self-Regulation

In Chapter 1, we explored the importance of leading with purpose. We're reminded that the leader and by extension the leadership teams' daily behaviours, routines and practices should embody the values and principles that they advocate. Similarly, when leaders are consistent, they don't just 'talk the talk' but 'walk the walk', this provides reassurance and security for the team. By setting a clear example, not only do leaders shape the culture, but they remove avoidance of doubt, so team members aren't left guessing about their motives or goals.

## Create Space for Experimentation

As we discovered in Chapter 4, innovation involves experimentation. In our profession, which is high stakes, this can feel like an unnecessary distraction and depending on where you are in your school improvement journey, you may have limited time and resource to dedicate to this.

If that's you, start small; think about what your zone of influence is and what you can realistically achieve. This might be a small and simple task, such as a knowledge sharing exercise, a safe space to challenge the status quo or engaging with wider reading and research through a critical lens.

When we're intentional about the desire to experiment and innovate, we create a learning culture that drives school improvement. Of course, this won't happen by chance. Those in leadership positions will want to consider how specific time and resource is allocated to this.

## Facilitate Open Dialogue

In Chapter 3, we explored the value of diversity of thought. This is key consideration when creating the right conditions for innovation. Teams with high levels of psychological safety and diversity of thought are not afraid to challenge traditional ways of working and the 'modus operandum'. Naturally, an integral aspect of experimentation and innovation involves failure. Leaders will want to consider how they prepare teams for this and develop their resilience. Inviting challenge and honest dialogue doesn't usually suffice, teams will need to have this modelled to them. When a leader can demonstrate this level of vulnerability, others feel able to follow suit. It creates a safe space for experimentation and calculated risk taking.

## Plan Ahead

If we don't plan for innovation, how can we be sure that it will take place? Innovative teams and organisations place a high premium on carving out time for experimentation. They clearly communicate this and protect and prioritise workstreams, so that team members have sufficient capacity and resource to try out new ideas. Some more forward-thinking schools are inviting experienced teachers to submit 'mini-research' proposals and where appropriate, enabling these teachers to have additional release time to develop their area of interest on the condition that they disseminate any new learning with the wider team. This way not only is the individual upskilled and professionally satisfied, the whole organisation benefits as they're encouraged to engage with research and become a learning community.

## Collaboration

There is power in partnerships. The explosion of professional learning networks and social media platforms, in recent years, means it's easier than ever before to debate specific approaches to pedagogy and share best practice. Therefore, irrespective of the context of your setting, location and governance arrangements, you have the oppor-tunity to engage with others. Even if your leadership team don't have an appetite for diversity of thought, as an individual you can widen your zone of influence, and that's liberating! Increasingly, we're also seeing professionals collaborate and use their collective voice to exert influence on educational policy.

## Stakeholder Engagement

Ultimately innovation should result in workable, scalable solutions. Give teams the best chance of success by encouraging them to engage with a broad range of stakeholders. Consider whose voice has not been heard? Are only the loudest voices heard? How have these stakeholders been selected? For example, are the same parent voices always shared? Are there more creative ways to seek out under-represented voices, for example through informal conversation on the gate, or local community events. Have you considered whether the method of communication itself is prohibitive? For example, are all families able to engage with online surveys, perhaps access to the internet or language is a barrier. How has our bias shaped engagement with stakeholders?

# How Do We Know If It's Working?

As educators, we don't need reminding that we have limited time and resource. We're required to report on a range of strategic priorities and demonstrate impact. Leaders will want to know if the calculated risks they've taken on more innovative workstreams are paying off. Stakeholders have a vested interest, and this information will need to be shared. Determine your key performance indicators early on, communicate this widely and measure regularly using a balance of quantitative and qualitative data.

As a sector, we benefit from measuring the impact of innovative workstreams and the work of innovative organisations so that this can inform policy, further develop good practice and support academic research into 'what works'.

───────────── **CASE STUDY 9.1** ─────────────

## One Life Learning

*This case study is informed by interviews with Dr Fiona Aubrey-Smith EdD MA(Ed) MMus FCCT FRSA FHEA, Director of One Life Learning, Founder of PedTech, and educator, researcher and author.*

One Life Learning, led by Dr Fiona Aubrey-Smith, works with schools, multi-academy trusts, professional learning providers and EdTech companies to transform teaching and learning. Named one of the Top 5 Visionary Women in Education in 2024, Dr Aubrey-Smith guides the organisation in promoting a pedagogy-first approach – 'PedTech' – challenging the sector's common 'tools-first' mindset and helping educators implement strategies that meaningfully improve pupil outcomes. Drawing on Fiona's award-winning expertise, research and publications, including *From EdTech to PedTech*, One Life Learning combines evidence-based guidance, professional learning and practical support to empower teachers while keeping pedagogy at the centre of digital technology use.

Many professionals still assume school improvement plans that include the use of digital technology, are underpinned by a robust teaching and learning strategy. However, all too often they're 'tools led', built around the capability and function of the software which is being introduced.

A classic indicator of this is a lack of engagement from the leadership team on how the digital learning strategy is being delivered. When all the responsibility is delegated to a subject lead with little or no strategic oversight from leaders, ambitious plans can amount to little more than a re-allocation of resource. Naturally, the ambition behind wanting to adopt or enhance digital learning is well intended; however, if a subject leader implements the use of software with little or no pedagogical reflection, this can lead to variable outcomes for pupils and unintended consequences.

Let's take the multiplication check, for example. Many schools have engaged with various platforms and software to prepare pupils for their statutory year 4 multiplication check. However, the way in which this software is implemented, directly contributes to pupil outcomes.

Often, schools and subject leaders will become aware of a digital tool that has had some level of success. Therefore, they choose to implement it in their own setting. Before long, all the staff have been trained in how to use the software and initially teachers report high levels of pupil engagement and enjoyment. However, if deeper pedagogical conversations are not being had about how and when it is best used, unintended effects begin to creep in.

In this instance we might find pupils who already have strong number fluency, recall and automaticity, enjoy using the programme and further develop their confidence. Those pupils who are not yet secure in their learning choose to have a go but make limited progress and those pupils who are struggling become thoroughly demoralised. This is then reflected in staff and parental engagement and after a period of initial excitement, the software is deemed to be 'no good'. Of course, the digital tool itself is not the issue, but rather its deployment or the absence of any pedagogical discussion around how it supports the teacher to deliver the key teaching concepts.

Hence, it's time to 'flip the script', strong digital learning strategies don't start with the digital tool, they begin with meaningful discussion about our pedagogical intent and desired outcome. Once we've carefully considered the purpose of our curriculum design, through building a shared understanding and vocabulary, we're able to accurately diagnose what our pupils need, engage with an evidence-informed approach and move forward with a strategy that meets the needs of our context (EEF, 2024). This empowers teachers and leaders to make more equitable choices for pupils about how learning is accessed.

Fiona is keen to emphasise, when digital learning is employed in an equitable and dignified way, it has a substantial impact on school registers for pupils with SEND (Aubrey-Smith, 2023). This is exemplified through the work Fiona carried out with one academy trust based in Sutton and Surrey, where the number of children on the SEND register reduced by around a third because of embedded inclusive practice facilitated by technology. Learning became more accessible and those previously requiring SEND support were able to independently access learning through a variety of adaptive teaching techniques and digital tools. It serves a stark reminder that when everyone has increased access to digital learning (as opposed to just the pupils who have been identified having special educational needs), all pupils benefit. We're able to raise the bar for all through our universal SEND offer, diverting much needed resource to pupils with SEND that require a high level of targeted or specialist support.

*(Continued)*

The use of audio dictionaries also gave pupils working below age related expectations greater independence and autonomy. This has contributed to improved fluency over time. Typically, when a pupil doesn't understand a word, they must wait for the teacher, ask a friend or read 'around the word' (requiring the pupil to read many more words to find out the meaning of the unknown vocabulary). Whilst these traditional strategies can be useful for children to know, in practice when they're used, the pupil's cognitive flow and learning is inevitably interrupted. The trust's digital strategy has supported several positive outcomes, ensuring that the attainment of children across the trust is significantly higher than national averages and staff satisfaction is consistently 15%–20% above national benchmarks, positioning them as an employer of choice.

Schools looking to further develop their understanding in this area may want to consider:

- The use of digital tools: As acknowledged, when the starting point is a robust teaching and learning strategy, we can unleash pupils' potential and ensure pedagogy leads to equitable practice. This is particularly important when we consider the intersectionality of pupils from disadvantaged backgrounds and the systemic barriers they face. When there's consensus about how and when the digital tools can be used to facilitate learning, we're empowered to reduce teacher workload, redirect limited resource and improve pupil outcomes.

- Professional curiosity: All too often important discussions about what we teach and how we teach it, stay surface level. Fiona's research is a call to action. Are we ready to have challenging conversations about our deeply held pedagogical values and how we impart knowledge and skills?

- 'Screen time' is an excellent example. Across the sector there are some dominant voices on this topic. But are they always evidence-informed? How have we engaged with this debate ourselves? Are we triangulating data from a range of sources? Or do we prefer information that supports the view we already hold? Does confirmation bias creep in?

- Finally, when we talk about 'screen time' what do we really mean? Fiona explains, stakeholders are usually referring to passive use of screen time, for example gaming, 'doom scrolling' or addictive behaviours (many of which are being modelled to children by adults). But the ambiguity of language here, creates perverse problems when we start to label all screen time as 'bad'. Fiona presents us with an alternative way of articulating how we engage with technology (Aubrey-Smith, 2026).

- Occupy: (Stare and move) Screen time that simply occupies is passive screen time. When young people engage through watching, scrolling and viewing. The digital tool or device is typically being used for entertainment, as a reward or to encourage compliance.

- Activate: (Sense and react) Engagement that activates requires learners to respond to a stimulus, this might be a research task, a low stakes quiz, creating documents or presentations, or sourcing a video to learn a new skill.

- Challenge: (Think and enact) Engagement that challenges promotes the use of pupils' metacognitive skills, demanding that pupils think critically about their learning, applying their knowledge or evaluating, and synthesising concepts. This might include editing and improving tasks, interactive discussions and collaborative creative projects.

Sharpening our language on approaches to PedTech, is about far more than semantics. Paying careful attention to how we describe learning will pay dividends in the end. Over time, it drives behaviours, shapes policy and influences public opinion.

Ultimately, Fiona encourages us to think more deeply about what can be achieved and the role that PedTech has to play. What aspects of teaching can be automated moving forwards? What is the role of the teacher in steering, guiding and facilitating teaching?

We encourage pupils to step out of their comfort zone each day, but are we ready to take up the gauntlet, be that little bit braver and ask the difficult questions?

---

## CASE STUDY 9.2

### London South Research School at Charles Dickens

*This case study is informed by interviews with David Windle, Director of the London South Research School at Charles Dickens and Deputy Headteacher at Charles Dickens Primary School, leading curriculum development and innovation projects.*

Research schools aim to promote the use of evidence-based practices in education, helping school leaders and teachers implement research to improve pupil outcomes. The London South Research School at Charles Dickens specialises in supporting teachers to understand and apply research, particularly in areas that address the needs of pupils from disadvantaged backgrounds. As director, David Windle leads on innovation projects, partnerships and advocacy work delivered through the Education Endowment Foundation, ensuring that research is translated into practical strategies that enhance teaching and learning.

The EEF, was founded in 2011, research schools were established shortly afterwards to bridge the gap between educational research and practice in school settings. There are 33 research schools in total in England which form the Research Schools Network, a collective which has one central aim: to support schools to break the link between family income and education attainment through better use of evidence.

The London South Research School at Charles Dickens opened in 2019, having demonstrated their commitment to developing an evidence-based approach to pedagogy, access to a strong professional network and sufficient capacity and resources. The research schools are co-ordinated by the EEF and tap into much of their resource. An integral part of their work includes collaborating with schools in South London and the South East, and responding to requests for support. This includes training, exemplification and providing school-to-school support.

Advocacy is also integral to the work of the research school; therefore, leaders participate in outreach through regular training, webinars and blogs, and host several local and international visitors.

Naturally, the research school leads on several workstreams, however much of its innovative practice has originated from the EEF's Early-Stage Development Pipeline, designed to support

*(Continued)*

teachers and leaders develop ideas that are in their infancy. At Charles Dickens, this is exemplified through several projects, including Fluency Focus.

The programme has been carefully sequenced and consists of twenty one-hour whole-class reading lessons for Year 5 pupils, to be delivered once per week in place of an existing reading lesson. The lessons aim to improve pupils' reading fluency and consequently their comprehension of challenging texts. It seeks to address the challenges of poor fluency some pupils experience in Key Stage 2, which can result in poor comprehension and contribute to a widening attainment gap as pupils transition into Key Stage 3.

The work was developed and led by the London South Research school at Charles Dickens Primary. The team trained teachers and senior leaders to support with delivery and champion the programme. Participants received lesson resources and a comprehensive teacher handbook; this provided teachers with a clear structure for how fluency strategies were taught, modelled and practiced by children.

Participating teachers and leaders attended in-person training. Each school was also offered training webinars and coaching conversations. The programme brings together six evidence-informed reading fluency strategies to support the teaching of reading fluency:

1  Introduce unfamiliar vocabulary.
2  Modelled fluent reading.
3  Text marking and phrased reading.
4  Echo reading.
5  Paired repeated reading.
6  Reading for performance.

The programme was initially trialled with 10 schools; this was then scaled up to 20. The most recent EEF evaluation found that the programme showed promise in delivering its aims. Specifically, there was evidence of improved understanding, effective use of fluency strategies and fluency assessment among teachers, and teacher-perceived improvements in pupils' abilities to independently use fluency strategies to read fluently and more confidently. As a result, an efficacy trial will now take place with 100 participating schools.

David is keen to emphasise that the relationship between the research school and Charles Dickens Primary is integral to developing innovative practice. Workstreams such as fluency focus are, of course, borne out of an identified need and the daily challenges faced by teachers and leaders on the ground. Innovation is derived from classroom practice. Or as the old proverb suggests, 'necessity is the mother of invention'.

The research school and its associated programmes afford practitioners the time, resource and platform to explore new ideas. These projects provide the team at Charles Dickens with the opportunity to codify practice and develop emerging pedagogy. Programmes and resources that are developed are externally validated through rigorous EEF trials, so practitioners also benefit from extraordinarily robust quality assurance.

Codification and consistency of practice bring additional benefits, reducing teacher workload and improving teacher well-being. David explains – teachers need to be able to pick up a resource, readily understand its purpose and how to use it. Ultimately, we can innovate and create, but if new initiatives disproportionately add to teachers' cognitive load, then we haven't developed a workable solution.

Psychological safety has a role to play here, but perhaps not in the way we might imagine. Of course, practitioners need to feel as though they're working in an environment where they can take proportionate risks, but creating the right conditions for innovation requires us to prepare colleagues for failure. It's often these successive failures, and subsequent reflection, that result in innovation (See Chapter 4, Learning from Failure).

Whilst the research school leads on several different workstreams, all aspects of their work is underpinned by the mission to promote equitable practice, ensuring every child has the opportunity to reach their full potential, irrespective of their starting point.

It's human nature to resist change; when we're feeling overwhelmed or pulled in too many different directions, our instinct is to opt out, withdraw or stick to what we know. However, under David's leadership, the research school will continue to be an outward-facing organisation, he explains. 'It's about staying curious, staying humble and continuing to look for opportunities to learn from others… the opportunity to change'.

---

## ━━━━━━ LINKS TO CLASSROOM PRACTICE 9.1 ━━━━━━

There are some common themes within the case studies.

- In each instance what are the drivers for innovation at classroom level?
- What practical steps can teachers and school leaders take to foster innovation in your setting?
- How can the use of research and evidence-informed practices support innovation?

---

## ━━━━━━ THEORY FOCUS 9.1 ━━━━━━

### Open Innovation

Open Innovation was first introduced by Henry Chesbrough (2006), although originally intended for the business sector, there are many transferable principles for those working in education.

The concept of open innovation is very much rooted in partnerships and collaboration, an area in which school leaders are highly skilled. It suggests that organisations can further develop their practice by leveraging sources of innovation, both internally and externally.

Open innovation theory refers to three different models, depending on the direction of the knowledge flow that you wish to leverage. When applied to the education sector, this might include:

*(Continued)*

- Outside-in open innovation (or inbound knowledge flow): Schools interested in developing outside-in innovation, are often outward facing and place pupils and families at the centre of their work. Asking themselves, how can we best serve our community?
- They refer to evidence-based practice and research to develop their approach and establish relationships with education partners such as universities, charities and community groups to broaden their offer.
- Inside-out (or outbound knowledge flow): By contrast, inside-out practice is based on the belief that the strengths and qualities that already exist within an organisation will secure its future and ensure that this is sustainable.
- These leaders ask themselves, how have we progressed? What are we good at and what do we represent? What is our passion? They're interested in leveraging their strengths to compensate, or even better, eliminate their weaknesses. Increasingly these settings are also finding new ways to share their innovate practice, through social media, research and teaching schools and professional networks.
- Coupled processes: Increasingly schools are looking to develop outside – in and inside – out pathways to innovation. Making the most of external relationships and internal skill sets and protecting the time and resource for these to develop. This might be through strategic alliances and consortia or through professional bodies.
- These leaders are attuned to the needs of their community and centre the voices of under-represented groups, ensuring all stakeholders are heard. They're mindful of where their organisational strengths lie and where there are gaps in their knowledge and skills base, regularly horizon scanning to detect threats or opportunities.

### ━━━━━ LINKS TO CLASSROOM PRACTICE 9.2 ━━━━━

- Consider the three models of open innovation. Which model does your school setting typically engage in? Why?
- Can you describe a recent project or task which didn't go as planned or resulted in failure? What lessons did the team learn? How did this reflection help the team to make improvements?

## Summary

Creating a strong sense of belonging in an organisation can significantly boost innovation; this is amplified in inclusive environments where diverse ideas are shared and valued.

When employees feel connected, supported and seen, they're more likely to contribute creatively and feel comfortable expressing their perspectives. This, in turn, can lead to more innovative solutions and better decision-making.

This chapter looked at the variety of ways in which leaders approach innovation. We explored theories and research which describe the mechanisms for innovation and the impact this has had across the sector, improving the quality of education, improving efficiency and ensuring the education sector keeps up with changes in wider society. This is exemplified through the case studies of innovative practice in schools.

Societal changes are influenced by a range of factors, technological advancement, social movement and global events. Sometimes we choose change; sometimes it is thrust upon us.

How are we ensuring we prepare the next generation of thinkers and leaders for a future we don't yet know or understand? Are we able to be courageous, ask the challenging questions? Arguably as leaders our greatest gift of all is to consider how innovation can drive equitable practice.

## Reflective Task

Now that you've completed Chapter 9, take a moment to reflect:

1 One of the many challenges for leaders is that an individual's personal belief about whether it's safe to speak up is inherently subjective, making it difficult for leaders to create a universally 'safe' environment. With this is mind, consider how we're able to intentionally design workspaces and innovate workstreams that are underpinned by a strong foundation of psychological safety.

2 Consider RAG rating your team's capacity and ability against the six catalysts for innovation and psychological safety:

- Self-regulation
- Space for experimentation
- Open dialogue
- Thinking ahead
- Collaboration
- Stakeholder engagement

3 What evidence base will you use to support your assessment?

4 How will you triangulate this information?

5 How can this information help you to identify next steps as a team? How can this information be used to further develop the provision in your setting?

# References

Aubrey-Smith, F. (2023) *Changing learning, changing lives: What happens when EdTech becomes PedTech? An independent impact study for LEO Academy Trust.* Available at: https://www.leoacademytrust.co.uk/2801/pedtech-impact-report (Accessed 26 May 2025).

Aubrey-Smith, F. (2026) *PedTech: The impact.* Crown House Publishing.

Chesbrough, H. (2006) *Open innovation: The new imperative for creating and profiting from Technology.* Boston: Harvard Business School.

Department for Education (2025) *Curriculum and assessment review: Final report – Building a world class curriculum for all.* Available at: https://assets.publishing.service.gov.uk/media/690b96bbc22e4ed8b051854d/Curriculum_and_Assessment_Review_final_report_-_Building_a_world-class_curriculum_for_all.pdf (Accessed 26 November 2025).

The Education Endowment Foundation (EEF) (2024) *A school's guide to implementation.* Available at: https://educationendowmentfoundation.org.uk/education-evidence/guidance-reports/implementation (Accessed 26 May 2025).

Vincent-Lancrin, S., Kärkkäinen, K., Pfotenhauer, S., Atkinson, A., Jacotin, G. and Rimini, M. (2014) *Measuring innovation in education: A new perspective.* Paris: OECD Publishing.

Vincent-Lancrin, S., Urgel, J., Kar, S. and Jacotin, G. (2019) *Measuring innovation in education 2019: What has changed in the classroom?.* Paris: OECD Publishing.

# 10

# Place-Based Support

---

### Key Terms

These terms may be of use in understanding this chapter and subsequently facilitating discussions with colleagues in your school(s).

**Inter-institutional:** Between school settings/organisations

**Trans-institutional:** Beyond school settings/organisations

**Co-construction** is the act of collaboration or working in partnership working to achieve a shared goal/aim.

**Authoritarian** is favouring enforcing strict obedience to authority at the expense of personal freedom.

**Hyper-local:** Relating to or focusing on matters concerning a small community or geographical area.

**Theory of change** is a description and illustration of how and why a desired change is expected to come about, as a result of activities and inputs.

**Theory of place** is the rationale for working in a particular way, in a particular locality.

**Service user** is anyone who is directly impacted by a service, whether they're actively using it or have used it in the past.

**Opportunity gap** refers to unequal and inequitable access to resources and opportunities based on factors like race, ethnicity, socioeconomic status, disability or geography.

---

## Introduction

It sounds simple. Provide a high quality of education, provide a caring environment and support pupils to reach their full potential. But in today's climate, is that enough?

Schools play an important role as community hubs. This is in part due to the decline of public services which has led to an increase in leaders providing place-based support for pupils and their families (IFG, 2025). While many leaders are motivated by a moral imperative to serve their community, a tension exists. Schools are required to do more with less. In this complex landscape of budget cuts, a recruitment crisis and regular changes to educational policy, it's no easy feat.

This is further complicated by the fact that our education system has created unintended consequences. On occasion we've seen that an ambition to succeed at all costs has driven poor behaviours in leadership teams and in some instances, resulted in exclusionary practice.

Place-based support focuses on addressing local challenges by considering the unique characteristics and needs of a specific geographic area. This is achieved by tackling root causes of problems, promoting social inclusion and fostering sustainable development. Considered approaches to place-based support can help to mitigate the effects of structural inequalities and significantly improve life outcomes.

However, early help, intervention and place-based support can be a hard sell. We're distracted by the immediate operational demands of the job and there's very little guidance or practical support for leaders looking to adopt this way of working. But we know it works!

This chapter examines evidence and research which demonstrates how collaboration can transform lives and empower local people to respond to the effects of inequality. We explore case studies from leaders in the south and north-east of England who work in partnership with their communities to co-design solutions to hyperlocal challenges.

## How Can Research Inform Our Practice?

In Chapter 1, we looked at Maslow's hierarchy of needs (Maslow, 1943) in relation to leading with purpose. Maslow's principles can also be a useful way for school leaders to consider the needs of pupils and their families. The theory suggests human needs and wants can be organised into five tiers:

- Basic physiological needs (food, shelter)
- Safety needs
- Social acceptance and connection or a sense of belonging
- Esteem
- Self-Actualisation

Place-based support which focuses on strengthening communities and fostering a sense of belonging, can play a crucial role in fulfilling these needs. By creating opportunities for social interaction, community involvement and shared experiences within a local area, place-based support can help individuals to feel more connected.

Organisations work in partnership towards a shared goal or outcome, and these collaborations take place within the same locality to improve outcomes or living standards for the community. Typically, stakeholders and organisations from across organisations form alliances.

It's important to note, that whilst place-based support might take many forms (for example bid writing, infrastructure development or campaigning for policy reform), place-based support is much more than a term used to describe the way support is organised within a community. It's a movement; a way of thinking about 'joined-up' services, and a commitment to a collaborative, integrated approach where community leaders, third sector and public sector professionals work together to provide coordinated care for individuals.

Place-based support is unique and differs from top-down national programmes which are centrally funded by government or community initiatives that are independently run. It often involves organisations with responsibility for delivering statutory services and it's this partnership between statutory services and local voluntary and community partners, which enables a holistic approach.

The most successful examples of place-based support are continually reviewed and adapted over time. These adaptations are informed by the community members who engage with the service, empowering communities to have agency and autonomy over the changes and improvements they need, to achieve better outcomes for their locality.

## Why Place-Based Support?

Place-based approaches are not new and date back to at least the 1960s. During this period underlying social, economic or political grievances that led to clashes or protests brought about policy reform.

Early iterations included community development programmes and regeneration initiatives. More recently, the third sector have played a more significant role in place-based support. This is in part due to the displacement of families and increased poverty and deprivation. Funding to essential services was reduced over time; it became evident that local needs were changing, and the opportunity gap had increased (Taylor and Buckly, 2017).

## What Are the Benefits?

Place-based support promotes better outcomes by leveraging local resource, knowledge and community engagement. This directly contributes to improved health, well-being and quality of life. Hoole (2024) identified eight benefits including:

1 Collaborative decision-making: Partnership working within a specific locality can help to build relational trust, particularly when collaboration leads to greater transparency about how decisions are made. This can also result in greater 'buy in' and agreement from partners when decision-making occurs.
2 Resource sharing: Typically, there is greater sharing of knowledge and expertise, this is particularly important when resources are sparse across a region or within a sector. This way of working ensures maximum value for money and leads to cost efficiencies.
3 Strategic planning: When organisations collaborate to create place-based support and develop a proven track record of improving outcomes across a locality, the community develop confidence and trust in this way of working. This can promote further opportunities for strategic planning and result in increased stability, enabling community members to realise their collective goals.

4  Innovation: As we saw in Chapter 3, teams that bring together a variety of lived experiences, skills and expertise promote diversity of thought. We know that across industries, the highest performing teams demonstrate cognitive diversity; this contributes to innovative thinking and an increase in innovative practice.

5  Community engagement: Place-based support is focused on centring the voices and experiences of community members and those who engage with the services being provided. Community members are invited to shape the design and delivery of services, so that they're more likely to have meaningful impact and meet local needs.

6  Social inclusion: When place-based support is effectively delivered every effort has been made to engage with under-represented voices, boosting social inclusion and promoting equity of provision.

7  Emergency preparedness: The collaboration and partnership working that is necessary for place-based support to take root, promotes community cohesion. In the event of an emergency or a crisis, these are communities that may have more collective resilience, pulling together in times of hardship to address local challenges.

8  Crisis recovery: In the event an emergency or crisis does take place, it's often place-based partnerships that are at the forefront of recovery efforts, dynamically responding to local need.

## Barriers to Success

As experienced practitioners will attest, whilst this way of working is incredibly valuable, like most things worth doing, it can be challenging and at times uncomfortable. Partnership working requires open, trusting relationships that enable all parties to address difficult issues. This also requires us to be flexible in our thinking and to hold our views lightly, so that practitioners can be committed to ongoing reflection and adaptation.

The Institute for Research and Social Sciences (Munro, 2019) have identified the potential barriers to successful placed-based support.

## Power Imbalances

More localities are engaging in place-based support, however where insufficient efforts are made to engage with under-represented voices, there's a risk that power imbalances are reinforced. If it's only the community members who have always engaged in local change that continue to do so, their voice becomes amplified over time. However well intended place-based support is, a lack of diverse perspectives risks reinforcing systemic barriers of oppression.

## Expectations

As any leader will tell you, managing the expectations of a group with diverse needs and wants is a challenge in itself. However, it's essential to have honest conversations from the very onset to avoid disappointment further down the line. A frank appraisal of the situation will help all participants to have a shared understanding of what can realistically be achieved and the change that can be brought about as a collective.

## Accurately Assessing Need

Placed-based partnerships hoping to drive change in their community will want to work from a broad and balanced evidence base. This supports stakeholders to accurately assess need and prevent local issues from being mis-diagnosed. It's important to ask ourselves, 'What am I missing here? Whose voice is not represented?' to enable us to design solutions that meet the needs of all, rather than most or some of the community. We want to avoid the trappings of deficit thinking, identifying local strengths and developing innovative sustainable solutions for communities.

## Evaluation

Evaluation enables us to fully understand the impact and scope of any services provided. However, it's notoriously challenging to evaluate placed-based partnerships, in part due to the complex nature of the work carried out. Attempting to capture the impact of long-term objectives and measuring qualitative changes (such as changes to behaviour or rates of engagement) isn't easy. To help minimise some of these challenges, stakeholders are encouraged to co-produce an evaluation strategy, supporting partners to identify and capture long-term outcomes. This exercise will also inform strategic planning and enable leaders to build capacity.

# What Works?

There is a wealth of evidence that highlights the detail of successful approaches to place-based support. Broadhurst (2018) identifies the conditions required for successful cross-sector partnerships to flourish:

1  Common aims and a workable strategy.
2  Engaged partners with established levels of trust.
3  Effective leadership.
4  Strong governance arrangements.
5  Access to resources and skills.
6  Partnership history and a capacity for collaboration.

There's a need for partnership actions and local activities, supported by policies and funded beyond the short-term to help communities realise their long-term ambitions for the local area.

━━━━━━━━━ **CASE STUDY 10.1** ━━━━━━━━━

## Big Education

*This case study is informed by interviews with Liz Robinson, CEO and co-founder of Big Education, a multi-academy trust focused on transformative, community-centred education and leadership development.*

Big Education works to support schools across the country in rethinking purpose, culture and leadership. Co-founded by Liz Robinson, the trust provides projects and programmes that enable collaboration, challenge and innovation among educators. Drawing on Liz's expertise in capacity development and a client-centred philosophy, Big Education models practice in its own schools while helping others develop thoughtful, whole-child approaches that empower communities.

As mum to two young girls, Liz also works flexibly to manage her role. She advocates for and models an authentic, reflective and relational approach to leadership; creating cultures where it's ok to be a learner, talk openly about what matters and share challenges. This culture applies to staff, pupils and the parent community. The schools work hard to build trusting relationships so that parents can share whatever they need, from disclosures about domestic violence to immigration concerns.

The Big Education team have considered what this means for staff, encouraging colleagues to ask for help if they are struggling, shifting from a culture of 'proving' to one of 'improving'. Empowering leaders at all levels to have honest conversations ensures team members feel seen and heard, fostering a culture of continuous learning.

Liz is clear that every member of staff has the opportunity to further develop the culture of psychological safety; whether that's through interactions in the classroom, leading key stages, school leadership or system wide leadership across the sector.

The team have carried out extensive work embedding the school's values and ethos into classroom practice and the wider community, this is exemplified through 'values characters' that bring these ideas to life.

Pupils use the values to guide behaviour rather than following rules, with reflective practices enabling them to think critically about their choices and the impact on others, building self-management and an inner awareness. This is in contrast to managing pupil behaviour through compliance only.

The team at Surrey Square are encouraged to explore their relationship to risk, give others the space to make decisions and lead in their own right. Both children and adults have agency and are empowered to make good choices for themselves. This thinking is rooted in the trust's approach to equity, belonging and mattering and the belief that it's possible to hold space for everyone.

The trust's commitment to a holistic view of education has led to the development of Surrey Square Primary School's extensive community outreach. Situated on the Old Kent Road, pupils at Surrey Square are thriving, but this is often against the odds; inadequate housing and financial insecurity being top of the list of many complex challenges. Yet academic outcomes, progress measures and well-being indicators for both pupils are staff are high. Associate Headteacher Nicola Noble, has worked in partnership with the community, listening carefully to their wants and their needs. This approach avoids leadership teams imposing well-intended, but misguided, plans onto the community, based on false assumptions they may hold.

Nicola put the experience of under-represented voices at the heart of the decision-making process. This work has helped develop the Old Kent Road Family Zone (OKRFZ); a community hub co-created with families to make life safer, healthier and happier. It's also home to initiatives such as the monthly Marketplace. Once a month, on a Saturday morning, the school opens its playground, dining room and kitchen, main hall and early years space to everyone in the community. You don't need to attend school at Surrey Square Primary to enjoy the marketplace. In the main hall, families can pick up clothes, toys, fruit and vegetables and all items are free of charge. Throughout the day children can play, draw, chat and eat together. At lunchtime, everyone comes together to share a freshly cooked hot meal. In keeping with the school's commitment to working in partnership, the school employs a parent as head chef, who is ably supported by several parent volunteers. Similarly, after taking on board feedback from the community, the team introduced healthcare checks delivered by an NHS professional.

The space also holds several other events such as Youth Club which runs weekly, and 'Come Dine with Me', an evening for local parents and carers to come together, share food and enjoy a monthly meal, all free of charge.

Big Education are now running training to support other schools to work in similar ways, developing processes for community engagement that genuinely lead to co-production.

At Big Education, the team share four values:

- Be authentic.
- Be brave.
- Be curious.
- Be connected.

The leadership at Big Education have chosen values which demand a growth mindset and humility; values which imply leadership is a process or journey, rather than destination. Values which foster mutual accountability.

Driven by her own professional curiosity, Liz is interested in how we build capacity for the next generation of leaders, so that they have a healthy relationship with risk, intellectual reserve and access to a professional network, to enable them to be courageous and ask challenging questions.

As a sector we operate in a high-stakes culture; the absence of psychological safety can encourage leaders to ask unhelpful questions, such as how can we get these parents out of the way? How can we alter the curriculum with the sole aim of improving exam results? How can we attract more affluent parents?

Who do these questions really serve and why do we ask them?

At the heart of this is leadership. Liz is interested in the inter- and trans-institutional way leaders are being asked to lead and the expectation that they're now also required to be 'leaders of place'. Liz is exploring what leaders need, and how we best support them to be able to skilfully work in this way.

*(Continued)*

How do we encourage leaders to be tenacious and offer them the psychological safety and the necessary practical support? For example, how do leaders find the financial capacity and emotional resilience to do what's necessary at a time when the sector is so under-resourced?

More widely, Big Education's ripple effect can be felt across the sector. In keeping with the trust's commitment to equipping leaders for the challenges that lie ahead, Big Education have been carefully curating pathways they hope will lead to an alternative way of leading learning. They run several programmes and projects which aim to inspire, empower and support leaders to make change in their contexts. These include The Big Education leadership programme, a 2-year leadership programme, for innovative school leaders, and The Big 8, the core 'head, heart and hand' leadership toolkit. With a focus on powerful communication and personal vulnerability, this includes giving feedback effectively within a culture of unconditional positive regard, holding others to account, building, maintaining and deepening relationships and effectively managing emotions.

Their 'Rethinking Schools' project works with groups of around 10 schools over a 2-year period, to support sharing and joint innovation projects, resulting in a range of powerful tools for the schools but also for others to benefit from.

Liz and the team at Big Education have big ideas but appreciate that change comes from the many and not the few. The system needs change makers, which is why the team are dedicated to collating and amplifying the voice of others. With a dedication and focus on quality, their big ideas are coming, ready or not!

---

# ━━━━━ LINKS TO CLASSROOM PRACTICE 10.1 ━━━━━

The team at Big Education describe the high premium they place on psychological safety, in particular the importance of speaking up without fear of reprisal, being vulnerable and sharing challenges.

How is this achieved for:

- staff,
- pupils,
- families?

Big Education describe their values:

- Be authentic.
- Be brave.
- Be curious.
- Be connected.

How do these values support the psychological safety of staff and pupils?

Consider your school or trust's values. How are they being enacted? What (if any) influence are they having on the psychological safety of teams? The wider community?

## ═══ THEORY FOCUS 10.1 ═══

### Theory of Place

Theory of place highlights the importance of developing a deep understanding of the community within which we work.

This includes the unique characteristics and history of a location. We're encouraged to pay careful attention to the complex networks of relationships, shared values and social structures within communities. Places are not just locations but homes, with all the associated social, cultural, economic and emotional connotations you might expect. The theory suggests we have a responsibility as educators to understand the distinct identities and attributes of the community we're working in collaboration with.

Practitioners may want to consider:

- Place attachment: The deep emotional and cognitive bond that people have with a place. This is often characterised with positive feelings and a sense of belonging.
- Social capital: The shared values, relationships and resources that exist within a community and contribute to our overall well-being.
- Cultural commons: The shared cultural knowledge, skills and resources that are passed down through generations and contribute to the unique character of a place.
- Intergenerational knowledge: The transfer of knowledge, skills and experiences from one generation to the next, which is integral for building and maintaining a strong community.

## ═══ CASE STUDY 10.2 ═══

### Tees Valley Education

*This case study is informed by interviews with Katrina Morley, OBE, CEO of Tees Valley Education Multi Academy Trust, a system leader driving educational equity and Sean Harris, FCCT, an education leader and doctoral researcher at Teesside University, focused on reducing social disadvantage, promoting research-informed practice and supporting system leadership.*

Tees Valley Education (TVEd) is a multi-academy trust serving specialist and mainstream schools across the Tees Valley, committed to inclusive education, high-quality pastoral support and reducing educational inequality. The trust promotes social justice and excellence through a culture of commitment, courage, curiosity and care. Under CEO Katrina Morley and with the expertise of Sean

*(Continued)*

Harris, TVEd implements research-informed approaches, supports teacher education and fosters system leadership across its schools. The trust collaborates with strategic partners and research initiatives, including Child of the North, the N8 Research Partnership and the Centre for Young Lives, to co-produce place-based solutions that address the needs of disadvantaged pupils and improve outcomes at scale.

Their innovation (PLACE) aims to tackle root causes of poverty and inequality through hyperlocal initiatives, comprehensive community engagement and deep social listening to achieve meaningful educational and social outcomes across the Teesside region.

The drivers behind PLACE are intrinsically linked through people, place and policy. Sean explains people and partnerships are integral to place-based support. Careful consideration is given to how alliances are built, identifying strategically which organisations align with both TVEd values and mission.

As part of their wider mission, TVEd are committed to ensuring staff are upskilled and develop a deep understanding of the intersectional nature of poverty. For this reason, they're always keen to partner with hyperlocal organisations that can support with this work. Helping leaders broaden their view and move beyond narrow assumptions or a singular view about pupils' lives. For example, it might be true that a pupil doesn't have the right equipment for a lesson because the family are experiencing financial insecurity. But what barriers are that family facing? What are the systemic issues compounding this? Can we challenge ourselves to ask the hard questions?

PLACE refers in part to the immediate hyper local resource that's available and to alleviate some of the daily pressures for families, from food banks to uniform shops.

In keeping with TVEd's commitment to centring the experience of those from disadvantaged backgrounds, parents are invited to run a 'fair share' programme, ensuring families are empowered and able to make a dignified choice about how they support their children. It's a departure from traditional ways of working, or an authoritarian 'top-down' approach. Rather than designing programmes for the community based on misconceptions, families are invited to share intel about what they really want, resulting in tangible improvements to those who need it the most.

The team at TVEd are committed to developing an eco-system that seeks to address local priorities, including the local skills shortage. This has been a labour of love and TVEd now excel at building genuine partnerships between the education sector, third sector and private corporations. For example, local business leaders are regularly invited in to speak with teachers about what's missing in the sector, presenting educators with a powerful opportunity to better prepare children for employment opportunities and life beyond the school gates.

As local school leaders deepen their understanding of the complex and far-reaching nature of poverty, this thinking has influenced practice at school level. For example, Stuart Mayle (Headteacher at Brambles Primary Academy) recently identified challenges World Book Day celebrations were presenting for families. Parents and children alike thoroughly enjoyed taking part and the event was high on everyone's agenda. But with rising energy costs and increased costs for basic amenities such as groceries, a costume for World Book Day averaging £30 a piece was becoming a luxury that few could comfortably afford.

Armed with this tacit knowledge, Stuart and his team made some important changes. A plain white supermarket T-shirt was purchased for each child and classes were given fabric markers. In the build-up to World Book Day, pupils were given dedicated time at school and home to decorate their T-shirt. This meant that pupils were motivated to read the book and acquire enough knowledge about the characters that they could create their own design, promoting comprehension and inference skills and importantly, family time. As the school had already gone to great lengths to ensure all pupils had access to a range of books, World Book Day celebrations were able to be enjoyed by everyone. Initially a few parents had reservations about moving away from traditional celebrations, however the overwhelming majority supported the initiative and many parents reached out to Stuart and his team specifically to thank them for the change in approach.

Promoting equity and accessibility is always top of the agenda for the team at TVEd. Leaders are particularly skilled at co-designing and co-constructing initiatives with the community. For example, pupils have chosen to run a farm shop, rather than a food bank. Tuning in to the needs and wants of the community has enabled pupils to lead on projects they can take pride in.

The Trust emphasises the need to listen carefully to those with lived experience and work with the community to build programmes of support, co-producing and evaluating shared outcomes.

This is exemplified through the Trust's community magazine. Parents were clear that they didn't want a traditional 'Academy or Trust' newsletter, they wanted a magazine which reflected their child's experiences and the needs of the community. As a result, pupils from across the Trust co-author TVEd's newsletter. 'Junior journalists' capture events from across each setting, for example 'meet the author' events and sporting competitions. The magazine also carefully captures items of local importance. Pupils have interviewed property developers about local building projects, and the newsletter also contains a feature entitled 'Classroom to Careers' shining a spotlight on a local business and one of its employees.

Whilst a high premium is placed on local intervention, the Trust is also committed to addressing the wider systemic issues. Without this deeper work, the sector relies on 'band-aid solutions', rather than tackling the underlying causes. Hence Sean's relentless focus on policy and the systems and structures that reinforce inequity.

The team at TVed emphasise the power of 'ganging up on the problem, not each other', recognising that as a collective, educators are able to influence educational policy. Strategic partnerships have enabled the team to realise their goal of operating within an eco-system, collaborating on shared goals and challenging structural norms. More recently this has included working with the Child North East Policy Group to lobby for the auto-enrolment of pupils who are entitled to Free School Meals across local authorities and an end to the two-child benefit limit.

As winners of the Fair Education Alliance (FEA) Innovation Award, in 2024, TVed's long standing relationship with the FEA exemplifies how collaboration has enabled change makers to consider scalable solutions. Meetings take place through 'lead meets', at round table discussions and conferences where professionals from across the sector can share challenges and successes, upskilling through supportive challenge.

*(Continued)*

TVEd's executive team recognise that the challenges don't just lie beyond the sector, they also come from within, including the workforce itself. Teaching is a profession that doesn't typically attract those from other sectors. For many, it will be the first time they have been asked to problem solve and think about systemic challenges in this way. Of course, not everyone will choose this approach, but the team at TVed are determined it's their responsibility, as civil architects, to shine a spotlight on the structural and institutional barriers families face.

Leading with purpose and unapologetically hopeful, the team at TVEd are clear, educational inequality cannot be tackled through education alone.

## ━━━━━━━ LINKS TO CLASSROOM PRACTICE 10.2 ━━━━━━━

- At Tees Valley Educational Trust Sean and Katrina explain people and partnerships are integral to place-based support. How have the team worked hard to develop a 'listening culture'? How has this resulted in practical improvements for the community?
- What vehicles and platforms exist within your school or community to enable under-represented voices to be heard?
- Sean refers to the adaptations made to World Book Day, the farm shop and the community magazine, all of which centre the voice of the community. What opportunities are there in your setting for young people and families to positively shape and influence the provision or wider community services? Which local partnerships can support you with this?

## ━━━━━━━ THEORY FOCUS 10.2 ━━━━━━━

## Theory of Change

A Theory of Change (ToC) helps organisations to describe their long-term goal and the steps they need to take to achieve this. It can help practitioners to identify the potential impact of their work and manage risk.

This is achieved through creating a roadmap. The purpose of the roadmap is to articulate how and why the desired change is expected to take place. It also describes the context in which the work will take place.

The pathway is then 'mapped out', starting in reverse, beginning with the intended outcome, working backwards to identify each of the milestones and the conditions which will help to bring about change.

Practitioners are encouraged to think about the 'causal links' and demonstrate how planned activities relate to each other and why they will bring about change. For example, how do activities such as professional development, support for families with housing and parent workshops fit together and how will they contribute to increased knowledge and understanding.

When applied to place-based support, this roadmap will articulate the intended impact, activities and underlying mechanisms of change within a locality using cross-sector collaboration.

## Summary

Developing place-based support systems is a long-term endeavour. It requires significant time and effort to build strong foundations, establish effective partnerships and foster sustainable change within a specific locality.

It takes time to understand the local context, and it takes time to build relationships. It's this relational trust that is integral to the success of place-based support; however, it's also fragile.

Power imbalances and a lack of clarity around roles and responsibilities can hinder progress and risks reinforcing the systemic barriers that perpetuate disadvantage. However, intentional collaboration across sectors and strong stakeholder engagement at different levels can be transformative. Those different levels include:

- direct, personalised support to individuals.
- community engagement, fostering active participation.
- addressing local needs through partnerships and coordinating services.
- a systemic level, advocating for policy changes and system level reforms.
- wider systemic influences, engaging with cultural and social norms, economic and environmental factors.

Whilst approaches to place-based support are widely documented, there is less written about why place-based support is so necessary.

Part of the purpose of place-based support is to build capacity so that community can take charge of its own future, to speak for itself, build social capital and build connections within and beyond the community. Arguably this is needed now more than ever.

The research points to an urgent need for individual pupils and families to feel a sense of belonging. At a macro level, place-based support contributes significantly to our collective need for psychological safety and our sense of belonging. Particularly when support is co-designed and co-produced with the community, promoting inclusivity and resulting in meaningful impact.

```
 ── Reflective Task ──────────────────────────────────────────────
```

Now that you've completed Chapter 10, take a moment to reflect:

- How can engaging with a theory of change further develop your settings' approach to place-based support?

As a team, consider the following questions as a starting point:

1 What is the problem you are trying to solve?
2 Who are your key stakeholders?
3 How can you reach your audience?
4 What steps are needed to bring about change?
5 What is the measurable effect of your work?
6 What are the wider benefits of your work?
7 What is the long-term change you would like to bring about?

# References

Broadhurst, K. (2018) 'In the pursuit of economic growth: Drivers and inhibitors of place-based partnerships', *Regional Studies, Regional Science*, 5(1), pp. 332–338. https://doi.org/10.1080/21681376.2018.1530134

Hoole, C. (2024) *What is place-based partnership working and why is it important?* Birmingham Blogs. Available at: https://blog.bham.ac.uk/lpip/2024/01/11/what-is-place-based-partnership-working-and-why-is-it-important/ (Accessed 20 June 2025).

Institute for Government (IFG) (2025) *The precarious state of the state: Public services*. Available at: http://www.instituteforgovernment.org.uk/publication/general-election-2024-precarious-state/public-services (Accessed 20 June 2025).

Maslow, A. H. (1943) 'A theory of human motivation', *Psychological Review*, 50(4), 370–396. https://doi.org/10.1037/h0054346

Munro, F. (2019) *Place-based working*. Iriss. Available at https://www.iriss.org.uk/resources/irisson/place-based-working (Accessed 20 June 2025).

Taylor, M. and Buckly, E. (2017) *A historical review of the concept of severe and multiple disadvantage and of responses to it*. Lankelly Chase. Available at: https://e9a68owtza6.exactdn.com/wp-content/uploads/2018/11/Historical-review-of-SMD.pdf (Accessed 20 June 2025).

# Further Reading

Wolfe, T. (2024) *Place identity theory - examples and explanations*. Emotion Nest. Available at: https://emotionnest.com/place-identitytheory/ (Accessed 20 June 2025).

# Index